GLORY WRITERS

GLORY WRITERS

THE ART OF WRITING DIVINE CONTENT THAT GLORIFIES YOUR CREATOR

DEANNA DROGAN

NEW DEGREE PRESS

GLORY WRITERS

The art of writing divine content that glorifies your creator

ISBN   978-1-64137-316-6 *Paperback*

         978-1-64137-612-9 *Ebook*

CONTENTS

ACKNOWLEDGEMENTS PAGE

It's interesting how so many of us think that the concept of writing a book sounds like a simple and easy task. Even when I began on this journey and started writing my introduction, I thought *there is no way this is as tough as everyone says it is*. Fast forward months later and it's time to submit my manuscript of 10 chapters for copyediting, I was thinking a little differently. This book journey has been filled with a lot of hard work, strained eyes, and restless nights. Ironically enough this *is* a book written to *encourage* people to write, not *discourage*, but I mention the hard work that goes into it in order to get the point across that it really does take a village.

I will never be able to thank everyone enough who has supported me on this crazy journey. Whether it be the incredible people I was able to interview, all of my amazing editors and leaders from the Creator Institute, the people who pre-ordered my book--the list could go on forever. Thank you to every teacher and professor throughout my school years who helped me become a better writer and encouraged me to pursue my dream of writing a book. I am also beyond thankful for every spiritual leader throughout my life who has discipled me and pointed me to Christ in everything. Of course, I could not have done this or anything really without the love and support of my friends and family who mean the world to me. I am beyond blessed by the incredible people God has surrounded me with and truly am so undeserving. Lastly and most importantly, I would like to thank my sweet Jesus for putting this opportunity directly into my lap and using a disorganized, clumsy, goofy twenty-something, to accomplish His purposes. This journey has given me the incredible opportunity to hear from Him in ways I never have before and I can't wait to see what He does with it.

Listed Below are some of the very special people who had a significant part in making this dream become a reality:

Anastasia Armendariz
Joyce Bain
Emily Babbit

Jason Benham

Brian Bies

Kristin Billerbeck

Peter Carlo

Richard Cooke

Ron & Lisa Drogan

Thomas Drogan

Carol Fourre

Carolyn Fraiser

Danielle Gargano

Breanna Grant

Abby Hannon

Paula Harkey

Dr. Donn Headley

Jonathan Hickory

Qené Jeffers

Kimberly Kiker

Erik Koester

Carly Landgraf

Jessica Linker

Gloria McGee

Michele Moscatello

Ralph Moscatello Sr.

Ralph Moscatello Jr.

Stephanie Moscatello

Elizabeth Mowbray

Marcia Musgrave

Cheryl Nedrow

Caroline Nice

Cristi Nice

Samuel Nunemaker

Lorraine Perkins

John Putnam

Mary Quinn

Jessica Ramsey

Rebekah Seymour

Robert Shaw

Gina Sofio

Linda Stalls

Tess Stockslager

Cynthia Tucker

Kristan Wagenmaker

Lisa Whittle

Kristy Whittington

INTRODUCTION

———

"Whatever you do, work at it with all your heart, as working for the Lord, not for human masters, since you know that you will receive an inheritance from the Lord as a reward. It is the Lord Christ you are serving."

COLOSSIANS 3:23-24

I lay on my bed in my dorm room at Liberty University by myself in tears and confusion.

It was just another Thursday, yet it felt like anything but.

Hopelessness and doubt swarmed in like a flood, and my breaths became shallower and shallower.

I gazed out the window at the clouds that moved in quick and covered the only beam of light shining through my window. The room became dark, and so did everything else.

Okay, before you read any further, let me just pause to tell you that I promise this book is super uplifting. If you know me, you know I am someone who likes to have every light on in her house, whose favorite music genre is probably Christmas music, and who literally has a banner above her bed that says the word "happy." I don't do darkness and gloominess, but my teachers in every English or writing class I have ever taken have always stressed the importance of having a suspenseful hook, so I thought I would take a stab at it, okay? Let me continue.

To my surprise and quite possibly yours as well, this dark day I speak of actually very quickly turned into a bright one:

That Thursday was the day I felt God calling me to write a book.

In fact, this book.

Let me give you some context.

**

Hi, I'm Deanna (this is where you say, "Hi, Deanna"). I have struggled with anxiety on and off for quite some time now, and it was particularly bad on that dark Thursday. I was in my junior year at Liberty and that first semester was severely kicking my butt, to say the least. I was not sleeping much, not eating very well (no surprise here), and trying to balance working on the school newspaper staff and serving on hall leadership with taking eighteen credits, resulting in a not-so-mentally-healthy Deanna. That day, in the midst of chaos, I lay there feeling crushed and weighed down in defeat, gazing out the window to see nothing but dark clouds and no hope of a happy tomorrow. Amid a panic attack, which I had not experienced so badly since middle school, I suddenly developed this overwhelming feeling of urgency, like something had to be done—and I could not figure it out. The urgency was so strong, I began to feel it throughout my body, like a movement of heat traveling from my toes, to my stomach, to my head, and I immediately knew the Holy Spirit was communicating with me in some sort of way. I stopped to listen and heard a quiet whisper in the back of my head: "Write about it." The words penetrated my spirit to the point where there was no denying it, and yet of course, doubt came rushing in like a flood. "Write about it"—and I had a feeling the voice meant writing more than just a journal entry. Now, I have always loved to write, and writing a book had always been a dream of mine, but could that really be a reality? I felt the call so strong that day, but I had no idea how it would actually come to fruition.

Fast forward to a semester later: My schedule started to clear up, and so did my brain. I was enrolled in an inspirational writing course for the creative writing minor I had added. I was a journalism major, and don't get me wrong—I learned so much from my classes, even the ones that may or may not have turned my eyes bloodshot from editing on my computer after who knows what time. But with a passion for being witty and creative, I fell in love with most of my creative writing courses. During this particular course that semester, we were assigned the task of writing the first chapter of a book. Let's get this straight for a second: I have never been the type of girl to really enjoy school, but I thoroughly enjoyed this assignment—in fact, it was probably the first assignment I actually wanted to keep working on when I finished.

And that, my friends, is when I knew it had to be from God.

***

With the dark yet somehow bright Thursday from the previous semester in the back of my mind, I figured I would write a personal testimony of my battle with anxiety. I continued to write this book for a couple of weeks, with no hopes of it really ever going anywhere, until out of the blue I received a message on LinkedIn from the founder of the Creators Institute—a program geared toward college students to grant them the opportunity to write and publish their own books—asking me if I wanted to write a book. I had to stop for a second because everything seemed a little too good to be true. Here I am, trying to figure out how in the world I am going to be able to write a book, and then suddenly the opportunity just falls into my lap through a simple LinkedIn message?

So fast forward again to today and now. Evidently, I accepted the challenge. And here I am, writing my very first book, a dream of mine since I was just a little girl writing creative stories in my hot-pink-and-green composition notebook covered in pictures of my dog and favorite Disney Channel characters. This book shares a lot of my own personal story, but after really thinking and discussing with the professors and editors who have helped me along this crazy journey, I narrowed down the topic of my book to be about Christian writing itself. See, so many Christian books have been published about testimonies—whether that on overcoming anxiety or depression or challenging life events—and they are all amazing, but I've found that not too many books exist detailing the actual process of writing them. As someone who has always been passionate about faith-based writing, I wanted to learn, and the journalist in me wanted to investigate a little. As Christians, we read these impactful books or hear these moving Christian songs on the radio or watch these inspiring Christian movies (by the way, you know you grew up Christian if you have seen that one scene from *Facing the Giants* when Brock reaches the end zone) that do something to our hearts and cause us to want to change. But what is it about these pieces of creative content that produces this effect? What exactly went into the process of making them so powerful?

I may be stating the obvious here, but the process of writing a faith-based book versus a regular fiction or nonfiction one differs immensely, and I would say the primary difference is purpose. Writing any book sounds like a daunting task—even for those who enjoy the craft of writing. Every day, authors pour their blood, sweat, and tears into their work, often to end up spending more than they make. I recently came across an article in *HuffPost* titled "The Writer's Odds of Success,"[1] which taught me that even some of the most well-known authors of our time had to persistently fight for years to bring attention to their work. For example, it said, "Judy Blume, who has sold 80 million books, got nothing but rejections for two straight years. Dan Brown's three novels before *The Da Vinci Code* all had printings of less than 10,000 copies. C.S. Lewis got 800 rejections, and Western

---

1   Dietrich, William. "The Writer's Odds of Success." *HuffPost*, May 4, 2013. https://www.huffpost.com/entry/the-writers-odds-of-succe_b_2806611 (Oct.10, 2019)

writer Louis L'Amour 200. Even *The Diary of Anne Frank* got numerous rejections."

What's scary is that these authors dealt with the harsh realities of competition in the industry before many of the platforms we have today even existed. The same article references a poll taken from Pollsters, according to which 80 percent of Americans want to be authors. In today's day and age, so many platforms—like social media pages, blog sites, or website builder sites—make marketing fair game for anyone with access to an electronic device. In short, the field of writing or really any creative vocation such as photography, art, or music has become more competitive than ever before; in all honesty, I found myself a bit discouraged researching statistics about authors and book publishing to find more articles *discouraging* aspiring writers to attempt a book than *encouraging* them to. Each article had harsh truth to it that all came to the same conclusion: writing a book is no easy task.

***

But what if you completely changed your perspective? What if you decided to write for a bigger purpose than yourself? What if you came to the bizarre-sounding conclusion that the writing is not really about you, the author, at all? What if, instead, you made the bold decision as an author to write for Christ instead of yourself? Now, you might just think that sounds a little crazy, or you might even think that sounds a bit unfair. I mean after all, you are the one putting the hard work into your project, why should you not write for yourself? The beautiful reality, however, is that when we begin to shift our purpose from writing for our own gain or fame to writing to bring glory to the name of Jesus, being an author gets a bit easier. I am not saying the cutthroat competition of the field just randomly disappears into space, but suddenly the normal pressures the average author faces when attempting to publish dwindle away a bit, the harsh criticism from readers doesn't seem to hurt as bad as it normally would, and the aftermath of whatever happens with our work doesn't seem to stress us out as much. When we write for the glory of God, our work becomes all about Him and not us—a beautiful position from which we can enjoy the powerful, unique gift of writing to its fullest.

Throughout this book, we uncover several different aspects of successful Christian writing, all of which trace back to the concept of writing for the glory of God, ironically enough. But I want you to know that I don't want this to be just an average how-to book "for dummies." Rather than teaching you how to write a good book, my heart behind this book aims to help you position yourself as a writer in a place where you can best hear from God and experience the sweet communion with Him that I know can take place through the powerful act of writing. So many of us often underestimate the power of writing. Maybe it was ruined for you in English class when you had to complete that tough five-essay-question exam, or when you had to complete the writing portion of the SAT under an intense time crunch with that one kid smacking his gum and kicking the back of your seat over and over.

Even if you have never liked to write, I truly believe that it is a gift to us from God. You will find something special about releasing what is going on inside onto a piece of paper, into a journal, on a computer, etc. You might think, *Well, talking is also an outward release of what is circulating inside*, which is true. But with writing, you get to keep that release as a memory and look back on it someday in the future. You might forget what you said aloud. I know most of my own sentences begin with "What was I going to say?" because I have already forgotten before it has even come out of my mouth. However, with writing, you can always look back at that piece of paper as a memory to see what was going on in your heart that day, to see how far you have grown since then, and to see the amazing things God has done in your life through that powerful transfer from heart to paper.

Before you read this book, I want to emphasize that I don't have all the answers. This is, in fact, my very first book, so you might be asking what knowledge I even have on this subject. First off, I'll tell you this book features insight from some incredible and experienced Christian authors in the field, who I had the privilege of speaking with or whose teaching I have experienced from afar. Second, I have learned so much as I have gone through this process of writing a Christian book myself. Lastly, I truly believe that God called me to write this book for a purpose and has therefore given me specific content He wants to communicate to you through your reading—I am simply here to be His vessel. So as you turn the next few pages, I want you to cozy up in a comfy spot, light a candle (this step isn't necessary; I just have a thing for candles), and let these words soak in. I can't wait to see how God uses them to make you a stronger writer, a stronger creator, and most importantly, a stronger follower of Him.

CHAPTER 1

FOR THE GLORY

---

*"So whether you eat or drink or whatever
you do, do it all for the glory of God."*

1 CORINTHIANS 10:13

EXPECTATION VS. REALITY

The thought of writing a book may sound exciting. Seeing *your* name on the cover of a beautiful, fresh, hardcover copy of a compilation of *your* very own thoughts. Then envisioning yourself at your first book signing as the crowd filled with eager faces of fans awaits you and the paparazzi whip out their cameras and microphones. *We are ready for your close-up, Miss. Drogan!*

Then, of course, hearing the words: "And now please join me in welcoming Miss. Drogan, the *New York Times* bestselling author of *Glory Writers*," as you wave and blow kisses to your giant sea of fans outside the glass windows of the *Good Morning America* studio while you make your way over to take a seat.

Can you tell I dream a little big?

While dreaming big and pursuing the passions God has given you are important, you must also stay practical, understanding that while writing a book can be amazing, it is hard work that might not always bring you the results you imagined.

Let me pop my dream bubble and take a step back into reality for a minute.

The harsh truth about authoring any book is that the process is long and arduous, full of work that might not always pay off the way you hoped. In fact, writing a book often runs the risk of pouring your blood, sweat, and tears into a book, only to find yourself blowing off the cobwebs and dust in the back aisle of Barnes & Noble. This reality can be especially tough for Christian writers. Suddenly the battle shifts from an internal one to a frustration with God. You may find yourself wrestling with the question of why He has given you such an amazing vision and inspiration, to leave you scratching your head wondering why the public is not responding positively to it.

The truth of the matter is that the very second we, as Christian writers, begin to write a book for the glory or benefit of ourselves, we have already lost the difficult author battle—we can define this struggle as the battle of wanting to pursue your passions while worrying about the financial success aspect of it. In fact, the second we pursue any passion of ours without the intention of glorifying Christ through it, we make everything a billion times harder for ourselves. In fact, I'll go as far to say we were not even made to create for the glory of ourselves; we were made to reflect and glorify our creator. Matthew 5:16 urges us to *"let [our] light shine before others, so that they may see [our] good works and give glory to [our] Father who is in Heaven."* I don't mean to say that God does not want us to use the talents and abilities He has given us for personal enjoyment. He takes pleasure in our joy, but ultimately our calling is to serve Him and to bring glory to Him and His kingdom.

Think about it: if you want to write a book for the sole purpose of bringing fame and fortune to yourself and it ends up a complete failure, you will find yourself pretty upset that you failed to reach the high standard you set for yourself. That said, going into the process knowing that your writing is an act of worship for the purpose of glorifying God allows you to fully understand that whatever happens with your book—whether it sits in cobwebs or ends up becoming a major motion picture someday—it still was ultimately a success.

The author of books such as *Put Your Warrior Boots On: Walking Jesus Strong, Once and For All; The 7 Hardest Things God Asks a Woman to Do; and I Want God: Forever Changed by the Revival of Your Soul,* Lisa Whittle once found herself at a point in her career when she was about ready to quit writing once and for all. The speaker and founder of Ministry Strong, which equips leaders to preach the Gospel with integrity, prioritize family relationships, and learn proper soul care to serve Jesus with strength for the long haul, reached a point when she had been in the industry for a while and was starting to wrestle with things like numbers, and the lingering questions of whether she be a bestseller or not.[2]

"You go into it and you are very hopeful," Whittle said. "You feel like you are going to have the one book that becomes *The Shack* or a crazy success like that. Those books are really just one in a million, and it is mostly just a lot of hard work."

---

2   Whittle, Lisa. "Author." Lisa Whittle. https://lisawhittle.com/ (Oct. 10, 2019).

SHIFTING FOCUS

Her words immediately brought to mind me and my friends when we were younger. I have always loved to be creative, ever since I could remember, so if I had friends over we were bound to be creating a play, writing a song, or making some kind of video. One year, my friend Julia and I, as well as our little sisters, decided we were going to go all out and make an entire movie to enter into a Christian film contest. We had an inspiring idea: Julia would play an unsaved foster kid who gets moved to a home of Christians and ends up finding Christ. Boom—lights, camera, action.

As young middle schoolers, with little to no equipment and a cast of just five, including my dog, who was probably just about the best actor in the whole thing, I was convinced this twenty-minute movie would become the next big faith-based movie to hit the big screen since *Facing the Giants*. To my absolute shock as a seventh grader, our "masterpiece" of a movie, which I thought would place first in the contest, did not even place at all. Actually, to be honest, I don't even know if it made it into the contest at all. Our hard work, our minor disagreements on lines, hours of editing—all down the drain.

Now, of course, I look back and laugh, but at the time, I was frustrated and confused as to why my super-realistic dream of attending the Oscars suddenly went down the drain. This memory may not be the most serious of examples, but honestly, I often wonder: what if I just had enjoyed making a movie with my friends that shared the message of Christ? Would the approval of what some panel of film critics thought really have mattered as much? Or could I look back at the whole process as a fun and unique memory spent building my relationship with my best friends? Similarly, the book-writing process is an opportunity to create an intimate memory with Christ—a unique chance to pursue Him in a way we may not have ever experienced before.

**Back to Lisa.

"Things had gotten in the way of my passionate pursuit of Jesus," Whittle told me. "And in the process, it had really put a lot of turmoil inside of me to where I was getting eaten up by the desire for approval and all these things that really made me want to quit."

This season of discouragement and of wrestling with the Lord ended up teaching Whittle that the only way to get out of it was to only pursue Him harder, which ultimately became the inspiration behind her most popular and beloved book, *I Want God.* "I just realized that the only way I wasn't going to quit writing and the only way I was going to keep going in my career, no matter if I had success or I didn't have success, was to just desire God," Whittle explained. She realized that if she were just to desire God, the concerns and logistics that used to leave her questioning wouldn't really matter so much anymore. This realization really broke off a lot of spiritual and mental chains as she continued to pursue a career in writing. Now, Whittle expresses that she can truly focus on writing what God tells her to write and honor and pursue that.

Whittle's experience is a clear example of what happens when our focus is shifted from where it should not be and what happens when we shift it to where it should be. In fact, this principle does not even just apply to writing or any type of content creation, but really our whole lives as Christians.

When we keep our focus on the big problems in front of us, such as "I cannot seem to land that dream job I want," or "I can't find the husband that I thought I would have by now," or "no matter how hard I try, I just cannot seem to fit in," the problems only seem to grow bigger and bigger and end up standing directly in our faces, blocking us from seeking anything else. However, when we shift our focus onto Jesus Christ and look at Him, remembering that this life we are living is not so much about bringing glory to ourselves but rather about honoring Him in all we do, suddenly the concerns we once had somehow fall into place, even if it happens in a way we did not expect.

The scriptures tell us in Hebrews 12:2 to *"fix our eyes on Jesus, the pioneer and perfecter of faith. For the joy set before him he endured the cross, scorning its shame, and sat down at the right hand of the throne of God."* The enemy likes to trick us into thinking that stressing and focusing on our problems will somehow make them disappear; it is not so much that when we focus on God our problems always disappear, but rather that they somehow end up in the background since Jesus has been put in the center.

So, when you set forth on your book-writing journey, remember where to shift your focus. Remember that this project God has put into your lap is not really about your gain, but more about you being a vessel in the hands of a God who wants to speak to His people. God is not being selfish or mean; He is actually keeping in mind your benefit. While writing can be enjoyable and I am not here to tell you that your book won't reach high levels of popularity (nothing is impossible with God), being a Christian author, or really a Christian anything, is not all about seeing your name on the front cover of a New York Times bestseller, or blowing kisses to your fans as you walk up for that interview in Times Square. It's really not even about ourselves at all. It's all about God and bringing glory to His name.

RECOGNIZING THE CALLING

Romans 8:28 reads: *"And we know that in all things God works for the good of those who love him, who have been called according to his purpose."* I have always loved this verse—not only because of the comfort that God is constantly working all things for my good even when I can't see it, but more recently, also because of the absolute privilege of being called by God to further His purpose. See, the truth is He does not *need* me or you to accomplish His purpose, but He *chooses* to use us and to work through us in order to do so. How cool is it to think that a simple dream God places in your heart could be used for His ultimate plan?

So, how exactly do you recognize when a calling is from God or from our own flesh?

Christian author, pastor, and founder of DesiringGod.org John Piper defined a calling from God (specifically one to write) in his message titled "Has God Called Me to Write?"[3] as: "a work of God in our minds and hearts and abilities and relationships that results in a recurrent, not temporary; long-term, not short-lived; compelling, not merely interesting; benevolent, not selfish; Christ-exalting, not self-exalting desire to write, which proves fruitful in the lives of others. That is my definition of a calling to write. I will say it again:

---

3   Piper, John. "Has God Called Me to Write?" Desiring God. https://www.desiringgod.org/ (Oct.10, 2019).

It is a recurrent, not temporary; long-term, not short-lived; compelling, not merely interesting; benevolent, not selfish; Christ-exalting, not self-exalting desire to write, which proves fruitful in the lives of others."

Piper listed several reasons why anyone would desire to write. Writing is a sweet time to express yourself and let what is circling around in your head finally out onto paper. Writing is healthy! While I love to write faith-based material the most, I also do like to occasionally write about the everyday instances I tend to get myself in—and, let me tell you: there are many. For example, writing about the time I got pulled over for having a plastic bag stuck to the front of my car was a fun one. It went something like this: "Suddenly my stomach traveled up to my throat, which I did not even realize was possible as I slowly turned my eyes to face the police officer standing at my window and quickly popped the imagination bubble of my dad's face when I would tell him that I yet again had received a speeding ticket." I think I may or may not have just come up with an idea for my next book. Also, that was just one speeding ticket, might I say.

When I was younger, I used to write about almost *everything* that would happen to me. I remember turning a five-minute incident when my friend and I spilled nail polish on her bedroom carpet into what seemed like a motion picture on paper. I think it had to be at least five pages long. "Then, as we gulped deeply in the absolute sheer terror that her mother would send me home, we quickly thought of every possible solution to clean the pure red clumpy stain out of their fresh, new carpet in the upstairs hallway." Okay, so that may have been a bit dramatic, but it's just a glimpse of my passion! Writing can also be enjoyable, because whether you believe it or not, we were *all* designed to create. We were created in the creator of the universes' image, and boy is He a creative God! I think one of my favorite characteristics of God might just be His creativity. I mean, He created the giraffe, for goodness' sake. He expresses His character throughout His creation, in the same way we express ourselves through our creativity. This concept was explored by J.R.R Tolkein. According to TolkeinGateway.net, "'Sub-creation'[4] described the creative efforts of the Ainur, Elves, Dwarves, and the race of Men (including Hobbits), all of whom are themselves creations by Eru Ilúvatar or in the case of the Dwarves, by the ValaAulë and given life by Eru. It is called 'sub-creation' because original creation is the province of Eru alone, and that which is made by those created by Eru is derivative from the works of the One."

"We are makers by nature. It is properly satisfying to create things. And many people aim to make something beautiful by writing — something interesting, something compelling,"

---

4   "Sub-creation." Tolkien Gateway. http://tolkiengateway.net/wiki/ Sub-creation (Oct. 10, 2019).

Piper said. "And that is good, but that is not yet a divine calling to write. Just to have that impulse is not a calling." Here we can make the distinction between our own impulse and a divine calling. We must also note that this impulse to write is not always a bad thing. Like Piper and I mention above, God designed us to be creative. If you want to write something beautiful and compelling, go for it—but be sure to recognize what is a calling from God and what is not. *So, how exactly do you recognize this calling?* you might ask. I, for one, struggle here and there to recognize what is God speaking and what is simply my own thoughts and desires.

On several occasions, I have failed to do something God was calling me to do, as a result of getting caught up in the confusion of whether it was my own impulse or something divine. For instance, I was at church once and felt strongly compelled to speak a word of encouragement over a member of our church body. I just could not tell if that impulse was from myself or from God telling me to do so. That day, I found myself teary-eyed on my drive home in regret because I knew I had missed out on something God was calling me to do but had let myself get all in my head. I ended up texting the person hours later, but I still wonder if it had the same impact that it might have, had I been obedient in the first place, in person.

We can always recognize a calling from God if the calling is for the purpose of glorifying Him. See, our own flesh has absolutely no desire to glorify God. In fact, it finds it preposterous to glorify Him. Scripture tells us that the flesh and the spirit are actually enemies. Galatians 5:17 says, *"For the desires of the flesh are against the Spirit, and the desires of the Spirit are against the flesh, for these are opposed to each other, to keep you from doing the things you want to do."* John Piper beautifully defines the divine calling from God: "Then there is the impulse to write, not only to learn and not only to create something beautiful or interesting or compelling, but also the impulse to instruct and awaken and delight and transform people into obedient worshipers of Christ. When this impulse takes hold of a person, he is experiencing a call from God to write."

Okay, how powerful is that? Now that is an impulse no man or woman can receive on his or her own. It is Christ in us that gives us a burden for the world to make Him known. **What is super cool about that is that, to accomplish His purposes and draw His children near to Him, He will often use the specific callings that He places on each of our hearts.** Okay, wow, that was the Holy Spirit who wrote that, not me. As children of God, we are all called to make Him known to the people around us in our everyday lives, but God will often use the particular callings He places on our lives to do that through us.

"Then the impulse to write, to discover and learn, is never enough. It is good. It is real. But it won't satisfy. The impulse to make something beautiful and interesting and compelling is never enough. It is real and it is good, but it won't satisfy the person that has a divine calling from God on his life to write," Piper said. "A divine calling to write is a calling from God, through God, and for God. Until the writing is for God, it is not a calling from God. So we move from truth discovery through writing to creative expression — through writing to the role of a servant in writing — which I described earlier like this: the impulse to instruct and awaken and delight and transform people into obedient worshipers of Christ."

"Until the writing is for God, it is not a calling from God." This point is crucial. If you think God is calling you to do something that is glorifying yourself rather than Him, you may want to step back and do some discerning. Think about Jesus. Everything He did on Earth was to glorify the Father—every action, every miracle, and every conversation. We are to do the same. Also note that God's calling will look like an act of service. Like Piper says, you can definitely distinguish the difference between writing by means of impulse and writing by means of divine calling when the act becomes not just an activity but a service to the one we were made to glorify. If you are beginning your project, I am so glad and wish you the best on your endeavor. Perhaps consider checking the intent behind what you are doing. Are you working by divine calling or by your own impulse? I challenge you to take time and ask that God would speak to you and instruct you to the calling He has for you. Maybe spend more time in prayer or consider a fast. Whatever it is He has for you, you should be excited. You my friend, get to take a part in advancing God's purpose, for His glory.

LESSONS AND TEACHINGS:

- Dreaming big is okay, but remember that the chances of writing a NY Times bestseller are not always as large as you think.
- Our book experience begins to change once we shift from writing for our own fame to writing for the glory of God.
- Focusing on God during the book-writing process might not take away the common stresses book authors face, but it might give them a fresh new perspective.
- A calling from God to write is different from our own desire to. Neither is wrong, but you have to distinguish the two.

Here is a quick prayer you can pray before the next time you sit down to journal, blog, or write:

Dear Lord,
I thank you for who you are and the gift it is to write not only about you, but for you. I pray that during this project you

would fix my eyes on you and not on my own shortcomings. I thank you that whatever happens with this book, you would show me that it was not a waste because it was precious time spent serving you. I pray that despite how well it does, despite the amount of people who read it, despite the acclaim I receive from it, my biggest priority would be for it to be is pleasing to you. I also pray that Lord you would make the calling you have for me clearer than ever before. Speak to me and guide me on this journey that I am about to embark on. In Jesus' Name, Amen

CHAPTER 2

HEARING GOD & BECOMING HIS VESSEL

———

"For no prophecy was ever produced by the will of man, but men spoke from God as they were carried along by the Holy Spirit."

1 PETER 1:21

FINDING YOUR GOD NICHE

I have always had a passion for writing. From the third grade, creating stories about my dog being an undercover superhero (and, if I must say, Super Sammy was better than any superhero Marvel is putting out these days), to senior year of college writing feature pieces such as "10 of the best places to cool down with smoothies and smoothie bowls this summer," I have always loved creativity and putting words down on paper or in the computer.

In the summer before my junior year of college, I felt the Lord calling me to start a blog, where I would basically journal about some of the day to day, and delve into things that He was either teaching me or laying on my heart to share with others on a public platform. Little did I know that this experience would not just entail me taking my thoughts and putting them into a document, picking a pretty header picture, and pressing the blue publish button. It would involve a one-on-one conversation with God, an ongoing dialogue, a session of surrender.

John 10:27 says, *"7 My sheep hear my voice, and I know them, and they follow me."*

Can I be completely raw and honest with you? Sometimes this verse scares me—perhaps because I often don't think I can hear God as clearly as others can. Or, more truthfully, when I do hear Him, sometimes I cannot distinguish if it is Him, my own carnal mind, or even the enemy in disguise. However, when I write, His voice becomes clearer than ever before as the inspiration flows out onto the paper.

I believe that everyone has that special way, whether it be a talent, an activity, a passion, through which God speaks to them the clearest or the most. I'm going to go ahead and make up my own term and call it your **God niche**. This concept does not mean that you should put a limit on God to speaking to you in just one way, because He speaks in a lot of different ways. However, it is so beautiful when you find that sweet passion or that skill He has planted in your heart to give glory to Him—because often that is where we will hear Him the clearest.

Perhaps, if you chose to pick up this book, writing is that passion. Welcome to the club! Maybe you have never used writing before to communicate with God. I like to look at it as a form of worship. I remember a creative writing teacher of mine in high school once said, "I tend to feel a stronger connection with God when I write, than when I sing during worship at church." For some reason, at first I thought something was wrong with that, maybe because growing up in church, you kind of have this picture nailed in your head of what worship looks like—cue up picture of person standing in a pew with hands in the Rocky Balboa position and eyes tightly closed. I personally believe music is something uniquely special, but worshipping God can take many forms. We can worship through the ways we treat others, the decisions we make to go against the flesh and obey the word, and through our work and passions.

THE POWER OF A MIND AT REST

I remember one of my mentors in college saying she had a strong passion for doing laundry. "If you ever have laundry, send it over," she would say. The first time she told me that, I could not imagine how it was humanly possible for someone to actually enjoy the task of doing laundry—but that's coming from the girl whose hamper once broke from apparently exceeding the limit of clothes that fit in there. She went on to explain to us that she found laundry to be the special way she connects with God, meanwhile I looked at her as if she had two heads.

But, as she began to explain the concept of a mind at rest, suddenly it made so much sense. First off, I am a firm believer that when we put our minds to rest, whether through mindless activities, such as doing chores like laundry and vacuuming, or cooking, those moments are some of the most common and likely to hear from God. Think about it: we are humans and we are busy. I know, for me at least, my mind is typically racing on a day-to-day basis. *What should I wear today? What is for dinner tonight? Did that guy actually smile at me or was he looking at the person behind me (most likely the latter)?* When our minds are at rest, it is the perfect time for God to drop major truth bombs on us while He has our full attention.

can simply come with a pencil in hand, ready to hear what He wants to speak through you.

CHERISHING MOMENTS WHEN DIVINE INSPIRATION STRIKES

School was not always easy for me. I was not one of those students with a photographic mind like Cam Jansen who could glance at a study guide and then ace the test the next day. Studying, organization, and test-taking always seemed to take a huge effort, but with writing, I felt something different—especially when I would write with a God-centered focus. In fact, I recall times writing on my blog and looking back at what I had written to see words I know for sure I could not have thought on my own. *Like, since when do I use the word hence?* No, in all seriousness, on multiple occasions I have written on one passage of scripture I'd heard a billion times, and then, as I began to expound on them more, I learned through the writing process something I had never thought about before. When I actually put my mind to rest, it's almost as though God pours the content He wants me to say into my head and it simply flows out into the document. He teaches me through my own work. The process truly is effortless, because it is divine.

Divine inspiration is something difficult to explain. I would say you cannot fully understand it until you experience it

Second, the beauty of writing is that it can be a relaxing and releasing activity. It almost gives you the opportunity to just sit down and mindlessly unload the thoughts that have been rattling around your head for some time onto paper. Unfortunately, that is not the case when your hand starts profusely sweating and you keep anxiously gazing up at the clock as your grip on your pencil gets tighter and tighter while you struggle to write a four-page essay on *Of Mice and Men* that your whole grade depends on (this example may or may not be based on true life events). However, if you are simply journaling, blogging, or writing in any form that gives you room for creative freedom, such an activity has the potential to be relaxing and offers such an amazing opportunity to hear from God.

But here is the key that took me a while to really grasp—**if you want to hear from God, you have to stop trying so hard.** I honestly find it so ironic that we hear God often when our minds are resting. I think that kind of reveals a character-istic I love about Him: He is simple. Now, of course He is God—He is brilliantly complex in many respects, but He asks that we come to Him with a childlike faith. He doesn't asl for us to try so hard; He just asks us to simply come and b So, when you look to communicate with God as you wr remember to try to put your mind at rest. I know it is ea said than done, but remember that you do not have t down before your computer or notepad and try so hard for yourself. Author Lisa Whittle says on the topic of divine inspiration, "There is really honestly nothing else in my life like it, and it's one of the reasons I love to write so much because I love that time with Jesus. I love that it's such a sweet communion with the Lord." How amazing is it that writing, a simple activity, has the capability of becoming **sweet communion** with the Lord? When we write, our minds are put to rest, and we are fully surrendered what the Lord has to say.

CREATING A CLEAR PATHWAY FOR CONNECTION

God is always with us, and He is always speaking in unique ways. But what about the times when He feels so far away? What about the times when we feel disconnected from Him? Where does He go during these times? If He never left and is always by our sides, why do we feel times when we can hear Him so clearly, and other times when He seems to be on mute?

To be honest, I don't have one particular answer for that question, only because a number of factors can contribute, the majority of which are due to our own selves. For those of us who are in Christ, thankfully we have been saved from our sins through the death, burial, and resurrection of Christ, but our sinfulness can still get in the way of our connection with Him. If you feel that God is calling you to write a book, you must listen to what He has to share with you to write.

That said, you have to create a clear pathway not only for Him to speak to you, but also for you to be able to hear Him.

Unfortunately, our own sinfulness can prevent us from reaching the potential and living the abundant life God has called us to. That is a scary thought. That is why the enemy often disguises joy and satisfaction in the form of things such as idolatry, disobedience, addiction—all of which can become noise that serves as a barrier between you and God. Hearing from God is crucial at all times for any Christian, but for those in a position of leadership and influence over people, I would say a higher standard is necessary. Of course, none of us are perfect, and we *all* fall short of the glory of God, but a leader living in a pattern of habitual sinfulness while influencing the people around them is dangerous. Correct me if I am wrong, but I think that as authors, we are leaders. We have unique platforms to inspire and encourage our readers, which is truly an amazing honor, and not one we should take lightly. If we want to lead our readers through our writing, we must position ourselves to be able to hear from God. We must step into purity and examine and put to death whatever is getting in the way of our pathway for clear connection with Him.

We tend to forget to put to death several things that we do not always realize are sneakily causing more damage in our communication with God than we think. The media we choose to subject ourselves to, for example, often has serious consequences. Maybe you are filling your ears with music full of profanity or subjecting your eyes to TV shows that only welcome a spirit of perversion into a room. Media, while it can be used for good, is also a tool from the enemy to deviously and secretly keep God's children from mental purity.

I was honored that Jason Benham of the Benham brothers—authors, speakers, and serial entrepreneurs—took the time to share with me some of his best advice for writing an impactful Christian book (quick shout out to Liberty alumni for being amazing. Go Flames!). The brothers' book, Whatever the Cost, ventures into their professional baseball career, as well as their HGTV reality show, which was canceled before airing when, according to Whateverthecost.com[5], "the network succumbed to media pressures surrounding their faith." Though their TV show may have failed, God ultimately had other plans, as the brothers would soon go on to become #1 bestselling authors.

Jason said, on the topic of creating a clear pathway for connection with God as we write, "Everything starts with purity. You have to get to a place where you are pure before the Lord—no known sin, no roots of bitterness or unforgiveness

---

5   Benham, Jason and David. "Are You Ready to Live Powerfully?" Whatever the Cost | Benham Brothers. https://whateverthecost.com/ (Oct. 10, 2019).

toward others, no negative thinking or emotions toward others. You need to feel love towards your reader and write from a position of being a fellow traveler on the road. Make sure to take thoughts captive; don't let yourself get critical of anyone or even yourself as you're writing."

If you are going to take anything away from this book, that idea might just be what to remember. But I don't want you to interpret that as the need for your perfection. You are not perfect, and you never will be. The prosperity gospel teaches that we have the power to actually earn God's love, when the truth is, Romans 5:8 tells us that *"while we were still sinners, Christ died for us."* Nothing we did or can do will make God love us any more or any less; He is love, simply put. However, our misplaced priorities, impurities, and habitual sins can distract us and keep us from having clear communication with Him.

So, maybe this message is a bit of a wake-up call for you. Maybe you have been trying to hear what God has to say for a while, but you have felt like you lost connection somewhere. Do not be afraid to simply ask Him what is keeping you from hearing His voice. Interestingly, we often ask the majority of our theological questions to everyone *but* God. I don't know about you, but if I have a question throughout scripture, I immediately ask my parents or even Google before asking the author Himself. He loves us, He wants us to hear from

Him, and He will never speak to us with condemnation, but rather with gentle conviction. Romans 8:39-39 says, *"For I am sure that neither death nor life, nor angels nor rulers, nor things present nor things to come, nor powers, nor height nor depth, nor anything else in all creation, will be able to separate us from the love of God in Christ Jesus our Lord."* Now, nothing can ever separate us from the love of God, but we have the power to tune out His voice. So, tune in and position yourself in a heart of purity to hear from God, not just for the sake of writing a book, but for the sake of one-on-one connection with the Father who has so much He wants to share with you.

LESSONS AND TEACHINGS:

- Find your God niche: look for the ways you can hear God's voice the most. If it's writing, write. If it's music, play music. If it's art, paint.
- Put your mind at rest—it's funny how often we hear God the clearest when we are doing mindless activities or chores. When you write, be sure to relax your mind and give the Spirit room to talk with you. You don't have to try so hard; simply come with your pencil in hand.
- Look at divine inspiration as an opportunity to have sweet communion with the Lord.

- If you want to hear from God, make sure you are in a position to listen. Remove barriers and repent of any sin preventing you from hearing from God clearly.

Here is a quick prayer you can pray before the next time you sit down to journal, blog, or write:

Dear Lord,

I thank you for this beautiful gift of writing that you have given me. I pray right now that you would use it not for my own glory, but for yours solely. Please at this moment put my mind at rest so I am fully able to hear the amazing things you have to share with me. At this moment, I repent of any sin blocking me from hearing your voice as clearly as I should. Position my heart and my mind to be ready to hear what you have to share with me. Make me your vessel, oh Lord. I simply have the pen in my hand; I ask right now that you would speak through me. In your Name I pray, Amen

CHAPTER 3

WEAVING IN YOUR STORY

———

"As for you, you meant evil against me, but God meant it for good, to bring it about that many people should be kept alive, as they are today."

GENESIS 50:20

A NEW PERSPECTIVE ON THE BAD

Qené Manon Jeffers woke up in a cold hospital room disoriented, confused, in utter fear for her life. With no idea how she got there, she struggled to move as she gazed around the room at several unfamiliar faces and began to mentally accept the fact that she had been kidnapped.

***

Let me give you a little bit of context before this story begins to sound like a scary movie—because I don't do those. Ask me about the time my sister and I watched a scary movie, by coincidence on the very night the basement toilet started acting up. I remember lying in my bed, the only one awake in my house, hearing a loud banging sound coming from downstairs. Somehow I ended up waking up snuggled between my parents the next morning in their bed; I may or may not have been eighteen years old. Anyways, enough of that.

Qené is the author of A Peace Unfettered: My anthology of faith[6], a collection of stories about her walk with Jesus, starting all the way back with her salvation experience. The common theme of her book is her ongoing search for peace throughout her walk with Christ. "My search has been for peace ever since I became a Christian," Qené said. "Really, part of my story and how I became a Christian was that I was a very anxious and fearful person, so I have been on this constant search for peace that I find only in Christ. A Peace Unfettered just seemed perfect for the title of my book."

At the very end of her book, she includes a collection of stories centered around her near-death experience that took

---

6   Jeffers, Qené Manon. *A Peace Unfettered: My Anthology of Faith.* WestBow Press, 2018.

place about three years back. Let me tell you: Qené's story was one that brought me to tears—and I'll just put out there that I am not much of a crier. "My husband took me to a flea market after we got off work. That is the one thing we like to do to relax, but halfway through the flea market, I said, 'Pat, I am so sick; you need to take me home.' And he said, 'Well, would you want to stop for supper? We haven't eaten yet.' And I said, 'No, I need to go home right now. I am so sick,'" Qené recalled. "Well, I don't even remember that." The next thing she remembers is waking up in a hospital bed in fear, unable to speak or move due to paralyzing drugs, with no idea whatsoever that she had actually been placed on a ventilator in a medically induced coma for over a week.

"I thought that I had been kidnapped, bound, and gagged," Qené said. As she looked up in the hospital bed, crippled by fear, she watched various doctors walk by, but as she continued to scan the room, suddenly her fear began to subside as she saw a very familiar face standing by her bedside. "I saw Jesus standing at my bedside, and I asked Him, 'Is this to be the number of my days?'" she said. "And He said, 'Qené, whether it is or whether it isn't, you're mine, and I will not leave you are forsake you.' And so I knew that whether I lived or died, I was going to be okay." Having dealt with anxiety her whole life, this moment was pivotal, marking when Qené understood that Jesus was a very present God and never going to leave her, even up to the point of the worst possible fear we face: death.

But the story does not just end there—and I was so glad it didn't. As she continued to speak on the phone to me, I eagerly sat on my bed and wanted to shove popcorn in my mouth like I was watching a movie in a theater. With such a powerful story, God made it clear to Qené that she needed to share it with others. "One really neat thing God did for me is that He gave me curly hair," Jeffers said. "I have never had curly hair before." Now, you might be wondering what in the world a hairstyle has to do with sharing a testimony. But God revealed something amazing to Qené through this unique new blessing: "God said it was my mark, to remember the miracle it took to heal me from my illness, and when people comment on my hair, I can tell them about what Jesus did for me." Qené shared that she has had several people approach her in public places, such as the grocery store, to compliment her hair or ask her if her hair is naturally curly. "I always say no—it's supernaturally curly, because Jesus saved me from a near-death experience. Then I take about two minutes to tell them about Jesus, salvation, and healing, and what he wants to do for them," Qené said.

Holy cow—what a story the Lord gave Qené to share; I am fully convinced that while taking a simple walk in a flea market with her husband, she had no idea what was to come of that day and definitely no idea that it would result in a published book to share her story with the world. I still think about my phone call with her and imagine the peace of Jesus standing near her bedside. What a powerful story. But we should note here, friend, that *you* also have a powerful story to share. Maybe you didn't get supernatural curly hair through it (though I am still praying for that miracle for myself, as I look in the mirror at the hot mess of my own hair), but you still have a beautiful piece of God's story to bring to the table.

TRIUMPH THROUGH TESTIMONY

What continues to break my heart about the Christian community in particular is our lack of openness with each other, and I am speaking to myself here as well. We are told in scripture that our testimonies actually hold so much power, that they carry the capability of **triumphing** over the enemy. Revelation 12:11 says, *"They triumphed over him by the blood of the Lamb and by the <u>word of their testimony</u>."* We were made to share the things that God has brought us through with each other, which makes writing a unique and powerful opportunity. We can actually use our platforms to share the good things God has done in our lives and testify to His faithfulness to our brothers and sisters. What a privilege that we should not take lightly!

The truth of the matter is that we are drawn to other people's stories. This psychological phenomenon is what makes social media pages like *Humans of New York* so successful. I remember learning in my journalism classes at Liberty over and over again that the number-one thing readers like to read about are people and their stories. Even in photojournalism classes, we were taught that people looking at a newspaper would be drawn mostly to the images featuring the faces of other people. We love to learn about each other, I think because we love to relate with each other and come to the understanding that we are not alone. So, I don't know what message God has placed on your heart to write about. Maybe it is an autobiography, maybe a memoir, or maybe something focused on a particular topic, like a characteristic of God. No matter what it is, I want to challenge you not to be afraid to weave your own personal story into it. Let others know what God has walked you through. Our stories have power, because God is a powerful storyteller, and He is a faithful and good God who uses our hardships and struggles to impact the people around us—similarly to how Qené's story impacted me.

THE STORY BEGINS

In sixth grade, I walked through one of the darkest seasons of my life. To this day, I still get a chill up my spine recalling memories I have tried to block out my head for years. I will never forget the first night anxiety crept its way into my mind. I lay in my bed restlessly tossing and turning, mind racing, hands clammy, toes clenched as the fear of the unknown echoed through my bedroom. I got up and sprinted into my parents' room, tears streaming down my face as I held onto my mom as tight as I could—thankfully I was not eighteen this time. That night was the first time I had a panic attack, and it would not be the last. Day after day passed by of shortness of breath, shaking, and feeling trapped. I suffered embarrassment from my classmates, who witnessed me fleeing to the nurse's office on a regular basis. I think the nurse actually became my best friend at that school. Sometimes I would feel better and tell her I was ready to go back to class, and she would want to continue on with our girl talk—which I completely did not mind.

I had so many questions for God during this time of my life: *Where are you as I feel so alone and isolated in this struggle? Why won't you just heal me instead of having me visit these specialists seeking answers? What is the point of this pain, when I see absolutely no good in it?* After half a year of what I would call mental torture, my life completely changed one bright and sunny morning as I woke up actually concerned as to why I was not experiencing anxious thoughts for once. I lay there with my eyes closed in what felt like a half-awake dreaming sequence. It is hard to explain, but suddenly multiple Bible verse references began to flash through my head one after the other—the books and the numbers raced around my mind, and out of all of them, one reference continued to stick out in particular. It was Matthew 4:10, a verse I did not know. Having waited for answers for what felt like eternity, I immediately ran to the closest Bible in my house and opened to this chapter to read what it said. Sure enough, I opened my Bible to the time when Jesus is in the desert to be tempted by the enemy, and verse 10 reads, *"Away from me Satan, for it is written worship the Lord your God and serve Him only."*

In that moment, I came to understand that God was actually handing me over a weapon to combat the darkness I had been facing the past few months. When you continue reading on in Matthew 4, you come to find that each temptation the enemy threw at Jesus, He combated with the word of God, but after verse 10 the enemy gives up and flees from Him. After that morning of incredible revelation, I used that verse to combat the enemy's attacks, and while I am not going to say that I have completely removed anxiety from my life, it seems to be far in the background rather than close up in my face. I think this change happened because I know now that through Jesus, I have victory over it. God grew me in a lot of different ways through that experience. I grew a lot in my own confidence, and I definitely developed a stronger hunger to walk with Him, but I still often pondered why it had to be done through such brutal pain and hurting. Little did I know that God would give me an answer to my wonderings way down the road.

WHY IT HAS TO HURT SO BAD SOMETIMES

My freshman and sophomore years of college at Liberty, I was a part of the Eagle Scholars Program, an extracurricular program that taught Christian-based leadership. Honestly, getting into that program was a testimony in itself, because my SAT and ACT scores most definitely did not meet the requirements. Every year at the end of the program, the group would take a mission trip to New York City to spend the day in an inner-city Christian school in the Bronx. They would split into small groups to run different sessions for different grade levels of students throughout the day. Some groups did improv classes, while others did elementary school chapel or middle school gym. I signed up with the group that would be leading the girls seminar. I honestly had no idea what that entailed, but I knew my friends were doing it, so I just went for it. I came to find out that our group of six girls would have to find a topic to discuss in a room full of about 100 middle and high schoolers. Let me just get one thing straight: public speaking and I do not go together— hence an immense reason why I am pursuing a career in writing, but God sometimes (more like a lot of times) ends up having a sense of humor.

After going back and forth on what we wanted to share with these girls, we felt God was calling us to speak about common mental struggles that young girls deal with. Instantly, my sixth-grade anxiety nightmare came to mind, and I knew right off the bat that God wanted me to share it with the girls. *Great, I thought, so He wants me to not only speak in front of a large crowd of people, but also divulge an absolutely terrible memory. Awesome.* Come mission trip time, my group gathered in the school's auditorium and prayed before the girls filled in the seats. They just seemed to keep on coming in, and my pulse began to race faster and faster. As we prepared, we took a seat at the edge of the stage; I gulped and stared at a large crowd filled with girls texting, giggling, and whispering. My feet dangled on the edge of the stage as my friend who had opened up about her struggle with depression passed along the microphone to me.

"Good morning," I said. I took a deep breath and squinted my eyes to look into the crowd and saw hardly anyone even looking up. Insecurity came rushing in like a flood, making my face hot and red. "So, I want to talk a bit about my past struggle with anxiety," I began as I watched a teacher tell a girl talking to the girl next to her to be quiet. Then I began to share my story. From the beginning of the darkness to the beautiful morning that God changed my life through His word. Not to toot my own horn, but I ended up somehow delivering what I thought was an award-worthy speech.

Yet as I concluded the session for us, about ready to take a bow, the applause was not as loud as I had hoped and almost became one of those awkward silent scenes in movies involving cricket chirps.

Feeling as though I had made no impact whatsoever due to the lack of applause, to my absolute surprise, when we hopped off the stage and stood at the front of the auditorium debriefing on the session, multiple girls began to make their way up toward us. A few sweet girls came up to me with a sparkling hope in their eyes.

"Thank you for being vulnerable."

"I now finally understand that I'm not alone."

"My story is so similar to yours."

"Can you please pray for me?"

Hearing words like these just put a big, fat smile in my heart. No, I was not happy that these girls were facing darkness. That aspect broke my heart, but I was happy that they could relate to my story and they came to understand that they were not alone after all. Though I did not have much time to say all everything I wanted to say to them, as they had to get to class, I got to spend a few moments laughing with them, crying with them, and sharing more of my story. In those beautiful moments, suddenly everything made so much sense—why it had to be so hard, why I had to go through all that pain, why I felt as though God was just sitting there watching my tears. The truth is that He would use those tears to spark a light in the life of another struggling with that same pain. He loved these girls enough to watch me suffer so that I could bring a piece of joy into their lives.

AUTHENTICITY IS KEY

God has given us each a story to share. But our obedience in being authentic has the power to transform the lives of the people around us. After being able to talk to some amazing Christian authors, I have come to one particular conclusion: Authenticity is one of the most important, if not the most important, aspect to writing something impactful.

A clear example of the power of authenticity can be seen in entrepreneur, speaker, and author John Putnam's book *He Spends, She Spends: Why God Wants You To Live For Free*,[7] which seeks to help readers uncover the "why" behind their money choices and get them to a place in which their money problems are no longer a barrier between their relationship with Christ. When I read this book, I was inspired

---

7   Putnam, John. He Spends, She Spends: *Why God Wants You to Live For Free*. Fedd Books, 2016.

by Putnam's Godly wisdom that he offers in regard to our money choices, but also by his authenticity and vulnerability. Before giving insight to his readers, he first expresses to them that he has made just about every financial mistake in the book.

Understanding his story and his mistakes created so much more of a reader-author connection for me. Suddenly, John is not some expert out there in outer space who has it all together and wants to share this advice with people who don't. He becomes a human, who his readers can relate to and learn from, because they know he has been through some of the same or similar struggles they are dealing with. When I had the privilege of speaking with John on the topic of his book, I asked him just how important authenticity was in the process of writing his book and I absolutely loved his response. "If you want to print anything in your book, Deanna, about me and my opinions of all of this, I'll hope you will print this: it's that God's word doesn't need any help. It stands alone. It doesn't need my help. He doesn't need my interpretation. He doesn't need my stories. He doesn't need stories about mistakes and failures or successes, His scripture stands alone, first and foremost," Putnam said. "But I do believe that the reason that Jesus told so many parables in the Bible is that when people hear stories, and they read examples, they see themselves in the stories; they see themselves in the example and you're able to communicate, 'Hey, this is what this meant to me.' The authenticity in my opinion has got to connect back into God's truth."

Wow, I was blown away. How often throughout scripture does Jesus speak in parables that resonate with us so deeply and then end up changing our lives? They have that effect because we can actually place ourselves into these stories and relate to them. What if your story is the one that resonates deeply with your brother or sister and ends up changing his or her life? When we write, authenticity must be at the heart of what we do if we really want to impact people with the truth of God. Christian author John Acuff said, "The scars you share become lighthouses for other people who are headed to the same rocks you hit." Some stories and life events may be hard to open up about, but when we write, we are not writing for the gratification of ourselves. We are writing to encourage the people around us and most importantly to glorify our Heavenly Father. So, don't be afraid to share your story: God gave it to you for a reason, and it has the potential to change someone else's life.

LESSONS AND TEACHINGS

- God has given you a powerful story; don't be afraid to share it!
- As humans, we are naturally drawn to the stories of other humans.

- For some reason, our culture is under the impression that we must hide our hardships and struggles with one another, when truly our stories have the power to inspire and help those around us.
- Writing with authenticity is one of the key elements of making an impact on your readers.

Here is a quick prayer you can pray before the next time you sit down to journal, blog, or write:

Dear Lord,

I thank you for giving me my own story that is unique to me. Though I could not see the beauty in the moments of pain, I thank you for the things in my life that I have gone through that have led me to where I am today. I ask that you would use my story and my past hardships to be a light to those struggling with the same or similar situations. I pray that the words I am about to write would be authentic, raw, and pleasing to you. Though it might hurt to relive some of these moments, I thank you now that you have given me a new perspective to see that your hand was working all along and you will use them to let my reader know that he/she is not alone. In Jesus' name I pray, Amen

CHAPTER 4

DIVINE WORDS

"Death and life are in the power of the tongue;
And they that love it shall eat the fruit thereof."

PROVERBS 18:21

BLESSING THROUGH SERVICE,
NOT SERVICE FOR BLESSING

When I went on my first mission trip, to Costa Rica during my senior year of high school, I honestly did not know what to expect. See, I love to travel, but at the same time I tend to get a bit anxious. I was excited to see what the Lord was going to do through us, but I was not so excited for the plane ride, the housing situation, the food, the *bugs*—I may be the only one out here with an extreme fear of moths (if you are with me, maybe we can start a fear-of-moths support group and call it FOM). When we arrived at our housing complex, after a long flight and drive in a hot, sweaty van, it was definitely a lot better than I had anticipated but still would take some humbling. It resembled a prison in some sort of way, but also sort of a nice mansion if you closed one eye (and then possibly the other). I went on the trip not knowing many people but found myself sleeping on the top of a questionable bunk bed facing a very loud, dusty air vent in a tight room packed with six girls. Oh—and we shared one toilet, one that we were not allowed to flush. Talk about a bonding experience.

Now, I know I probably sound like a total and complete snob—I mean, what did I expect, to be staying at a Ritz Carlton on a mission trip to the poorest area of a country? No, but in my depraved humanity, I hate to say that I found myself complaining internally here and there. Little did I know that God would use that trip to change a lot in me. I knew going in that I was ultimately there to be a blessing to His people, but in fact I, even in my sinfulness and imperfection, would be the one to ultimately receive the blessing. The first day we spent praying with families in a very poor village was the very first time I saw a house made of cardboard boxes, which immediately pulls at your heart strings. Over the course of the next few days, we visited different orphanages and heard some of the heartbreaking stories of the precious children there. Some were horribly physically and mentally abused by their parents, while others were just abandoned and left unwanted. We got to spend a lot of time playing with them and doing some handiwork around the orphanage facilities.

I found the trip painful, both physically and emotionally. I had a little boy at one orphanage cling to my leg everywhere I walked. I would turn around and look down to see his little grin and sparkling eyes gazing up at me. Leaving him and getting on that bus to go back to the housing complex that day was not so easy. But seeing the joy in each child we came in contact with touched my heart in a way I had never experienced—I think because it was a different joy than I had ever felt before. Here, these kids had absolutely nothing, had been abandoned and severely hurt by the ones they looked up to the most, yet they ran around with genuine smiles on their faces and still showed us so much pure love. Maybe that meant my worst day didn't have to be so bad after all.

On that trip, I truly discovered that when we are serving Christ—even if that looks like getting our hands dirty, sharing one toilet, or even having to ward off evil moths—He ends up ultimately blessing us through whatever we are doing in His name. The same goes for your writing. We talked about how writing can be used as a tool for worship in the previous chapter. If you are serving the Lord through your writing, most likely you will find that He will bless you in the process. That said, I'm not exactly sure what that kind of blessing will look like. On my trip to Costa Rica, it looked like the contagious joy I caught through the beautiful people we met. However, what I do know about *your* blessing is that it will be beautiful, even if the process looks broken—like parting ways with a sweet, motherless little boy who followed you around an orphanage and made you smile so hard you couldn't stop.

I want to make it clear that I am not encouraging you to write to receive a blessing, but to understand that though the task of writing a whole book may be daunting, ***if God is calling you to it, He will not only bring you through it, but will grow you through it***—and it will be a beautiful thing. If you follow me on Instagram or any social media platform, you might gather that I am a big fan of the *New York Times* bestselling author and founding pastor of Redeemer Presbyterian Church in New York City, Tim Keller. Keller posted on Instagram once, "The fear: If I obey God, I will not be happy. This is the same lie that Satan told in the garden." Often, God will call us to do things that cause us to step outside of our comfort zones for His glory. The enemy sits back and tries to convince us that our obedience to God's calling will not be worth the inconvenience. That said, I fully believe that no greater reward exists than that which comes when we take that leap of faith and pursue the action God is calling us to.

GROWING THROUGH YOUR WRITING

I had the honor of speaking with the author of *Break Every Chain: A Police Officer's Battle with Alcoholism, Depression, and Devastating Loss; And the True Story of How God Changed His Life Forever*,[8] Jonathan Hickory, and of hearing a bit about his book-writing process. I admire Hickory's boldness and willingness to delve back into some deep-cut wounds throughout his life to point others to the hope and renewal that comes from Christ's restoration. When he heard the call to write from the Lord, he obeyed it, and despite the exploration back into the darkest of days, God blessed him through his willingness. "I've always enjoyed writing, and I definitely enjoyed it when I was younger, you know, in college and stuff, but I certainly never thought of myself writing a book," Hickory said. Hickory believes that God told him clearly to write his book. Walking out of church to his car one day, a man in his men's group stopped him and randomly said, "Man, I feel like you are going to write a book." "After he told me that, I feel maybe he had some prophecy gifts, because God laid that on my heart at that point and I just couldn't shake it," Hickory said. Although Hickory found victory over strongholds in Christ's power *before* writing his book, he said that *through* the process of writing his book he actually received a fair amount of his healing. With his

---

8   Hickory, Jonathan. Break Every Chain: *A Police Officer's Battle with Alcoholism, Depression, and Devastating Loss; And the True Story of How God Changed His Life Forever.* Covenant Books, 2018.

obedience to serve through his writing, he received blessing by means of his own spiritual growth.

"I grew a lot in my knowledge of Scripture, and what it meant," Hickory said in regard to the process of writing. "It was also really healing to me, because I had a lot of trauma in my life and to lay that all out fairly, openly, and honestly actually had great healing power. It was almost like through the baring of my soul, God began to equip me to comfort others. My book is a memoir, so looking back I was able to see how God was working in my life at times that I had no idea. To see the awesome power of God, when we're clueless, and also to just see the character of God—how he really, really loves us. But that doesn't mean the discipline us if we are out of line," Hickory said. Hickory's story is a testament to many things, but for our purposes, it highlights the power of writing and the power of words. Wow, if we actually understood the power words hold, I think we would find ourselves speaking or writing with more positivity, more encouragement, and more life. In Hickory's case, the words he wrote down actually held healing power for himself.

Here we can see what a unique gift the ability to write is (and, news flash: anyone can do it). Writing can be a very powerful experience and beautiful opportunity for significant self-growth. Importantly, though writing for the Lord is a service to His kingdom, don't feel like you are being selfish if you want to gain something from it too. I am not talking in terms of money or fame; I am talking about the desire for the same deep spiritual change, growth, healing, etc. that you are hoping to bring to your readers. In fact, that is the beauty of the whole Christian writing experience. We have this special opportunity to grow closer to the Lord than we ever have before by spending intimate time with Him and learning through the gift He has given us to write. Even if God is calling you to write or create something challenging, like a book about a past struggle, or maybe a blog that will require a fair amount of research—trust in Him, trust in His promises, trust in His character, trust that He does not only care about the audience you are writing for, but He cares deeply about you too as the author. Don't take your time writing for granted; see it as the precious opportunity it is: a time to glorify Christ and grow deeper in your relationship with Him.

WORDS OF AUTHORITY

Recently I have gotten into personality tests, though I do believe they are often taken a bit too far. I know that they do not define me, but I find it fun to get to know some of the deeper reasons behind the decisions you make. Oh, and no, I am not talking about stuff like the "What kind of *Friends* character are you?" on Buzzfeed. I have taken my fair share of those, and I get Joey every time (not sure whether to be happy about that or deeply concerned). I am talking about the ones that ask you the deeper questions and actually make you start thinking about yourself. For instance, I just figured out that I am a type nine on the enneagram test. After this realization, I suddenly did not feel so alone in my utter fear of being the designated person to choose where to go out to eat, or make any decision on behalf of a group. Making decisions is not exactly my forte.

Another personality test I like is the Love Languages test founded by author Gary Chapman. My number one love language is words of affirmation. That came as no surprise to me. My absolute favorite thing is opening up a letter someone wrote with me in mind. I'm not sure if I am the only one like this, but when I receive a letter, I *rarely* open it up right after I retrieve it. I actually savor it and wait to open it at a time when I am all by myself in a spot where I can focus on it and cherish every single word without being interrupted in any way. I like to make it a sweet moment between me and the person who wrote it.

During my time at Liberty University, I served on dorm leadership for two years as a small group leader. I recall our final leadership team meeting as my junior year was coming to a close: we sat in a circle around our group leaders' cozy dorm room and we each were given a sheet of paper to write our name on top of. We were then instructed to pass that sheet around in a circle to each member of our leadership team, and they would write a sweet little note about you. I remember directly after that meeting holding onto that piece of paper, not taking one peek at it as others looked down and secretly glanced at theirs as they walked out. I, on the other hand, kept my head up as I walked upstairs back to my room, limiting any temptation, hopped on my bed, and assumed a comfortable position before I took my time to read each generous note with a huge smile on my face. The words written down did something to me. They changed my entire mood that night. Maybe I am overly sentimental, but I must say, even if your number one love language is not words of affirmation, words do something to all of us—and, really, that is not just an assumption, but a Biblical fact. God actually tells us that both death and **life** are in the power of the tongue.

I hate for you to reflect on a bad memory, but can you think about a time someone said something that hurt you? I guarantee you never forget it. I still remember standing in line as a fifth grader in the hallway at my elementary school and whispering something into my friend's ear in front of me, though we were supposed to be quiet and "on our best behavior." The second I slightly opened my mouth to whisper, a teacher materialized out of nowhere, came right up to my face, and said these words in a harsh tone: "You think you're special? Because you are not. Nobody is allowed to talk." Okay, so maybe I was overly sensitive as a fifth grader, and maybe I should not have been talking when I was not supposed to, but at twenty-two years old I still remember that exact moment, to the point where I can even remember I was wearing this dorky green-and-red fleece that made me look like a Christmas elf that my mom had always pressured me to wear. Words stick with us, and they have the power to either build us up or break us down. Ephesians 4:29 says, **"Do not let any unwholesome talk come out of your mouths, but only what is helpful for building others up according to their needs, that it may benefit those who listen."**

A CHANCE FOR CONVERSATION

Though we are not necessarily speaking audibly to our readers when they read our work, we are essentially having a unique conversation with them. This statement might sound a little nutty, but I am sure you can relate. When I read, I often feel as though the author is speaking me—I can almost hear them in my head, in a way. I have been reading Lysa TerKeurst's book Uninvited, and the relatability of some of her stories is actually insane, almost like she puts you into her mind in each situation she finds herself in. Reading is truly a unique, intimate experience between the author and the reader without them physically being in the same room. How interesting is it that through a book I can know some of the deepest darkest areas of someone's life or maybe some of the highest, brightest mountain tops without having ever met them?

For example, I attended Elevation's women's conference this year, *Reflect*, led by the amazing Holly Furtick. As the worship began at the start of the evening, I scanned the audience only to notice that one of my favorite authors, Levi Lusko, was sitting in the crowd with his wife. I recently had the privilege of reading his book *I Declare War: Four Keys to Winning the Battle with Yourself.* Lusko candidly opens up about his struggles with anxiety, depression, and narcissism throughout this book, and it is beyond powerful. However, at the conference, I immediately started fangirling the moment I saw him. After the conference, I felt almost an obligation to go say hi to him, as if we were like lifelong best friends, when the truth of the matter is that I have never in my life met him but just happen to know and relate with some of his deepest, darkest struggles through reading his book.

Bestselling Christian author Max Lucado said in his piece "The Write Stuff"[9] that "written words go to places you'll never go … and descend to depths you'll never know." What an amazing privilege we get to embark on as Christian writers. We get to be communicators. Throughout this book so

---

9   Lucado, Max. "The Write Stuff." MaxLucado.com https://maxlucado. com/writing-corner-tips-tools-aspiring-authors-artists/. (October 10, 2019)

far, I have talked about how we are creators, because we are created in God's image, and He is creative. But another brilliant aspect of God is that He is a communicator. He speaks to His people in unique ways—whether through His word, through nature, through thoughts, through others, the list is endless, really. As people designed in His image, we must build our readers up, as the scriptures tell us to do. We must use words to change the progressions of our brother's and sister's days. We must let them know that we care and that they are loved by their perfect Father above. Most importantly, no matter the circumstance, we must point them to Jesus. I love the way Lucado describes the incredible opportunity at stake when our readers pick up our books: "The readers invite the author to a private moment. They clear the calendar, find a corner, flip on the lamp, turn off the television, pour the tea, pull on the wrap, silence the dog, shoo the kids. They set the table, pull out the chair, and invite you: 'Come, talk to me for a moment,'" Lucado said.

With that in mind, talking to our readers lets us speak life to them. Let's craft words of encouragement for them. Let's put smiles on their faces as they sit down in their favorite spot eager to hear from us. The coolest part of this whole thing is that if we are being messengers of Christ as the authors of the scriptures were, we are fostering an intimate moment not only between us and our readers, but more importantly between them and God. That should be our ultimate goal in this whole process. "So accept the invitation. We need your writing. Pick up the pens left by Paul, John, and Luke, and write for the souls—they show us how," Lucado said. So, whether you are writing or whether you are speaking, never underestimate the power of words. For goodness' sake, God created Earth by speaking things into motion—words hold a lot of power. God's words hold the most power of all, so let's position ourselves to hear what He wants us to share with our readers so we can be the communicators He created us to be.

LESSONS AND TEACHINGS:

- When we obey God and serve Him, we will experience the fullness of His blessings and our own spiritual growth.
- You should write not only to impact your audience, but also to impact yourself as the author as well. Look at writing not just as an activity, but as an opportunity to grow in your walk with the Lord.
- Words hold serious power. God tells us that death and life are held in the tongue. Use the words you write as encouragement and to always point your readers back to Jesus.
- Look at writing for an audience as an opportunity to have an intimate conversation with them. What would you want them to learn/know about God, themselves, you, etc.?

Here is a quick prayer you can pray before the next time you sit down to journal, blog, or write:

Dear Lord,
I thank you that you find joy in putting a smile on my face—that scripture says you think so many good thoughts about me and you dance over me. As I write today, please change my perspective, so that I can see this as not just a chore or a simple hobby, but an opportunity to serve you. I pray that through this process you will be teaching me, helping me grow me in different areas, and using me to bring words that point my readers back to your Son. Speak to me and allow me to be the encouraging communicator you designed me to be. In Jesus' Name I pray, Amen

CHAPTER 5

LAYING IT ALL DOWN

———

"Watch and pray so that you will
not fall into temptation. The spirit is
willing, but the flesh is weak."

MATTHEW 26:41

THE ART OF SUBMISSION

The flesh is weak. If this statement is a surprise to you, I would like to get some tips from you. I don't know about you, but I am struggling right now as I write these words down. Everything in me wants to crawl into my bed on this chilly day and binge-watch a hundred episodes of *Fixer Upper* while I know deep down that I need to be wise, discipline myself, and actually get the things done today that I need to accomplish.

Our flesh is weak, and often in more harmful ways than the desire to watch sweet Chip and Jo fix up old houses. Scripture tells us that apart from Christ we can do nothing. John 15:5 says, *"I am the vine; you are the branches. If you remain in me and I in you, you will bear much fruit; apart from me you can do nothing."* With that said, you might ask, *How in the world are we supposed to write content that has the power to transform lives?* Well, I hate to break it to you, but we unfortunately do not have that ability. We do not have that sort of wisdom, and we most definitely do not have that kind of power. But, before you think this book was written to crush your hopes and dreams, I want you to know, friend, that the God we serve is merciful enough to delight in using us in all of our weakness to impact the people around us in huge ways. Scripture tells us that the Spirit is willing to work through us!

Though the Spirit works in us in all things, we have to do our part—and here is where the act of submission comes into play. Submission sounds like an easy task, but if you are anything like me, you like having a sense of control over situations. If we are being completely honest here, the desire for control is something I struggle with on a day-to-day basis. I often put so much pressure on myself to be everything to everyone, when in reality only Christ can do that. I constantly have to remind myself that I do not have the power to change someone else's heart. While I can play a vital *part* in guiding them to their transformation, God ultimately does the transforming. Letting go and surrendering to that fact is a challenge I continue to pray that God will walk me through.

I fully believe that feeling as though we *need* control is really one of the most common lies the enemy uses for our destruction. Failing to submit to God's control in our lives puts the pressure of the whole world on our shoulders—a place it was never meant to be. Colossians 1:17 tells us that **"He is before all things, and in him all things hold together."** *That* should take some weight off.

When bad situations hit us, as humans our first instinct is often trying to discover a way that we can fix it. Sometimes God gives us the direction and ability to do so, but what about the situations that we have absolutely no control over? What about the times a grandparent or loved one gets diagnosed with cancer? What about the times a sister decides to turn to the bottle or a drug? What about the times when we find our own selves caught in the evil cycle of anxiety and can't seem to find a way to escape our own minds? We can pray for situations like these and take the necessary steps in obedience to get help or help one another, but is there really anything in our human power we can do to restore them or heal them completely?

Fortunately, the answer is no—and I use the word "fortunately" intentionally here because, believe it or not, the biggest of blessings is that we don't have to put that massive amount of pressure on ourselves to handle impossible situations and can instead trust a loving, all-knowing Father who has what is best for each of us. **In our minds we think that surrender makes us weak, but in fact it gives us more power than we can imagine.**

Do we have the ability to change the hearts and minds of the people who read the books we write? No, we do not have that type of power or control, but God does, and He is willing to work through us. If we want to write a book of eternal significance for our audience, we must humble ourselves before our Father and put our project completely into His hands, saying, "Lord, I can't, but you through me."

SURRENDERING THE STAFF

A Christian author and pastor of Saddleback Church in Lake Forrest, California, Rick Warren highlights surrender as one of the key components of hearing God speak in his message titled *Hearing the Voice of God*[10]. "Now, to hear God's voice you have to start with an attitude of submission," Warren said. "You surrender in advance. It's not like 'Tell me, Lord, and I'll decide what to do.' It's a matter of 'I have already decided yes; now tell me what the instructions are.'"

Warren then brought up the story of Moses at the burning bush in Exodus chapter 4. Verses 2 to 3 read, Warren described: "Then the Lord says to Moses, 'What is in your hand?' 'A staff,' he replied. Moses is out in the wilderness and he is tending sheep, and one day he sees this burning bush and he walks up to it and the voice comes out of the burning bush and says, 'Moses, this is holy ground. Take off your shoes.' So Moses takes off his shoes. Then God says to Moses, 'What is in your hand?' God says, 'Throw it down,' and it becomes a snake. Something that was dead comes alive. And then he says, 'Pick it up.' And he picks it up, and once he does, it becomes a stick again—it just dies. Now, is that not the strangest story you have ever heard?" Warren asked. "'If you give it to me, I will make it come alive. I'll do a miracle with it if you give it to me and lay it down. But every time you pick it up and you take it back it is going to die. It just goes back to dirty, old, dead stick.'"

---

10   "Hearing the Voice of God with Rick Warren," YouTube video, 49:00, "Saddleback Church," Jul 7, 2015. https://www.youtube.com/watch?v=-MkxaUoFPbw

To be honest, while I always have thought this story in Exodus was super weird, I often overlooked it. I had never thought about how much revelation is actually compacted into this short, very odd moment in Scripture. When we surrender and put things into God's hands, they come to life, but when we hold on to them and keep them for our own control, they die. Think about it: the moment Moses takes the stick out of his own hand, lets go, and places it before the Lord, it comes to life. But the very moment he picks it back up, it dies. We as Christian writers can look at the staff as our upcoming projects. When we let go and give God full reign over them, we can expect them to come to life; however, the moment we seek full control, they die.

The enemy wants us to believe the lie that we know what is best for ourselves and we can live our lives on our own. But if the flesh is weak, and if without Christ in us we can do nothing, how do we expect to create things that will come alive? The concept of submission means understanding that the one who breathed life into us in the first place is saying to us, "I've got this; you are simply my vessel."

"After this happens in Exodus 3 and 4, never again in the Bible is it called Moses' staff," Warren said. "From this point on, every time this stick is mentioned in scripture it is called the rod of God, that God uses to do all the miracles in Exodus. He does all the ten plagues with the rod of God. Moses takes the rod and dips it in the Nile River, and it turns red as blood. He holds up the rod of God at the Red Sea, and it splits. Every single miracle from that point on was done through the rod of God. What is in your hand?"

All the amazing, pivotal moments in biblical history that actually impact us today through Moses' simple act of obedience to submit and lay down that rod should absolutely blow our minds. "This simple little story is one of the most important stories in history, because if this had not happened, there would be no Exodus, there would be no Ten Commandments, there would be no nation of Israel, there would be no Messiah, there would be no death on the cross, and there would be no church, if Moses hadn't have done that," Warren said.

I don't know about you, but I want God to make my book come alive. I want many pivotal miracles to be enacted through my book. But I know that I do not have the power to make that happen on my own—only Christ through me holds that power. Therefore, I choose to place my book down on the ground before the one who is strong when I am weak, the one who knows when I know not, the one who brings to life what is dead inside of me. Do you?

LETTING LOOSE AND ENJOYING THE RIDE

Writing a book is a big project, and if you are anything like me, you tend to get in your head a bit. When I write, I begin to think that absolutely every single word has to be perfect, which will usually result in one of two outcomes: I will either procrastinate to avoid the stress by doing something mindless like binge-watching a TV show, planning my Pinterest wedding for endless hours, or taking a trip to the pantry every time I am at a loss for words, *or* I will end up writing but not enjoying the process as I gaze out the window dramatically wishing I was elsewhere.

I know for a fact how fun writing can be. Many of my friends may think I am a dork for saying that, but if you are passionate about writing, you know that no better feeling exists than when that random burst of inspiration strikes you (most likely a late hour in the night) and you find yourself getting absolutely lost in the words that begin to flow out of you like a river. I went through a week of severe writer's block recently. It wasn't until 1 a.m. on a Wednesday night as my head was going down to hit the pillow that God decided to suddenly bombard me with the endless inspiration I had been looking for. I shot up and whipped out my computer, and let's just say I did not get much sleep that night.

Friend, you should enjoy the passions and gifts that God has blessed you with, not dread them. Enjoying anything can be difficult when you are putting loads of pressure on yourself to make sure it is absolutely flawless, which is why it is crucial to put out your absolute best work, while remembering that perfection is simply unachievable. Don't beat yourself up over mistakes—you are only human! Thankfully, as Christian writers, we can look to a perfect, all-knowing God to work through us. Our job is to surrender and trust Him. Throughout this book, we have talked much about this common theme of writing for the glory of God, a concept that not only allows you to glorify your much-deserving creator, but one that also takes the pressure off when it comes to things like success, numbers, publicity, and money. When we choose to write for God and not for ourselves, our perspectives change for the better. For some reason, I think when we think of God asking us to do something, our minds immediately go to something extreme like packing our bags and flying off to a dangerous country where no one speaks English and having to shower with a bucket. Now, do not get me wrong, maybe God actually is or has called you to pack your bags and fly off to a dangerous country where no one speaks English and shower with a bucket. He is a God of adventure and humility and will often make us step out of our comfort zones. But He also might ask us to serve Him in simple ways that He designed us to enjoy.

It is very hard to comprehend how much God loves us and delights in us. Unfortunately, I personally believe we each have some level of a distorted image of love due to the imperfections of the people around us, here on Earth. We find it hard to fathom that God can love us so perfectly despite ourselves and shortcomings. I love Zephaniah 3:17, which speaks of the great delight God finds in us. It reads, *"The LORD your God is with you, the Mighty Warrior who saves. He will take great delight in you; in his love he will no longer rebuke you, but will rejoice over you with singing."* This should motivate us to not look at our writing as a chore to slave over, but as a privilege to let loose, relax, and enjoy the project He has set before us! Don't waste the process. Cherish each moment spent with your creator and each concept He brings into your head while putting forth your best work. You don't want to end up with a finished book in your hand someday, looking back and feeling as though you had wasted the process. Rather, create a memory of you joyfully serving your savior.

Christ came to give us life abundantly. We were not designed for a boring, average life. Well-known author Joyce Meyer said in her devotion titled "You Can Enjoy Your Life-Every Day!"[11] that John 10:10 is "an absolutely amazing scripture because it clearly tells us that God doesn't just want us to be alive, but He wants us to enjoy being alive. He wants us to live

---

11   Meyer, Joyce. " You can Enjoy Your Life--Every Day!" Joyce Meyer. https://joycemeyer.org/everydayanswers/ea-teachings/you-can-en-joy-your-life-every-day (October, 10 2019).

with joy—abundant, overflowing joy!" Meyer says in order to get this abundant joy of the Lord, we must abide in Christ and make everything in life revolve around Him—including your next project (I added that last part). But, if our books truly revolve around Christ, how can we not experience joy? Joy is one of God's characteristics, and it might just be my favorite one, but it doesn't just bring a smile to your face; it actually brings a smile to your heart.

That may just be the corniest line I have ever written in my entire life.

But if you have experienced the joy of the Lord, I think you understand that the joy is not temporary—like the joy of opening up a gift, or seeing a friend after a while of living far apart—but rather satisfactory and unexplainable. "I've learned through my own experience that if you don't have joy, then no matter what you have or what you do or how great your circumstances may be … it doesn't mean much," Meyer said.

I don't know about you, but I want my writing to mean much, and not just the final product, but the process and everything in between. I want do it with passion and enthusiasm, and I want that to come across clearly to my readers. But, while I want it to mean much to my readers, I also want it to mean much to myself. I want to enjoy this process and this sweet time of communion with the Lord.

Not every second of writing will look like a fine and dandy walk in the park. You may experience frustrations and hardships throughout the writing process. But I love this quote from Meyer: "Make a decision today to enjoy your life. If you're too serious about everything, lighten up! Learn to laugh at yourself and the things that normally frustrate you. Remember that God loves you always. He knows everything about you and loves you anyway."

Not every moment of the book-writing process is going to be pretty. Think about the times you are faced with writing about a really dark time of your life and unwanted memories begin to flow back. Or think about times when you have too much going on but know that a deadline is coming up soon. For me, that time is right now, spring of 2019, as I am literally packing up my townhouse, graduating, saying goodbye to my home of four years here at Liberty University, and waking up at weird hours to get some writing in. Frustration comes easily, but if I actually take a second to comprehend the fact that I am writing a book—that God has actually given me this incredible opportunity to serve Him by doing something that I love—how can I not be joyful?

"It's important to understand what joy is. It's not about enter-taining yourself all the time, getting your way all the time, or laughing all the time. Joy can be extreme hilarity or calm delight and everything in between!" Meyer said. So take this amazing opportunity and enjoy it. God has obviously led you to this project and given you certain passions and gifts for a reason.

LESSONS AND TEACHINGS:

- Because our flesh is weak, we need to practice full sur-render and submission to Christ, asking Him to write content through us that can transform hearts.
- In Exodus, when Moses laid down his staff before God, it was brought to life, but the moment he took it back into his hands, it died. Similarly, when we surrender our work into the hands of God, he will bring the words to life, but if we try to do it on our own, it will lack trans-formative power.
- Don't view your writing as a chore to slave over, but more as an amazing opportunity to serve our giver by practic-ing what we love to do.
- Don't let perfectionism steal the joy out of writing; instead be reminded that serving God means serving joy, because that is one of His characteristics.

Here is a quick prayer you can pray before the next time you sit down to journal, blog, or write:

Dear Lord,

Thank you for the gift of writing. As I sit down with my hands before this keyboard, or my pencil in hand, I come before you in a posture of surrender saying I cannot, but you can through me. I ask that you would write content through me that has the power to transform hearts and minds, because only you can. I choose to lay down my work before your feet, asking that you do with it what you will. Allow me to take the pressure off myself to make this perfect, and instead use this opportunity to practice what I love to do. I thank you that you delight in me and love to see me happy. You are such a good Father. It's in Jesus' Name I pray, Amen

CHAPTER 6

THE INVISIBLE WAR

―――

"For we wrestle not against flesh and blood, but against principalities, against powers, against the rulers of the darkness of this world, against spiritual wickedness in high places."

EPHESIANS 6:12

HEADING INTO BATTLE

Believe it or not, we are in an unseen war as we speak, and the secret to winning a good amount of that battle is understanding that very fact itself. Think about it: if you head into war with little to no knowledge of what to expect or who you are fighting, how do you expect to position yourself for victory? If you are going to be writing or creating something that glorifies God and will move your audience, you need to understand that the enemy is not going to like that. News flash—the enemy doesn't like God, and he doesn't like you, hence his least favorite combo is you doing things *for* God. Now understanding that spiritual attacks are often inevitable should not scare us. In fact, it should empower us—because the truth is that we have already won the battle or, rather, Jesus won the battle for us the day He beat death on the cross on the grounds of Golgotha.

If we are in Christ, we are walking in victory over *everything*, including death. 1 Corinthians 15:55-57 reads, ***"O death, where is your victory? O death, where is your sting? For sin is the sting that results in death, and the law gives sin its power. But thank God! He gives us victory over sin and death through our Lord Jesus Christ."*** So, knowing he is defeated, the enemy works by way of deceit and will do everything in his power to make you feel like you're on the losing side. I am not sure what spiritual warfare will look like for you; it could be a mental battle, like depression, doubt, or insecurity, but it could be an external one, like a form of a physical sickness. It is important to know, however, that as Christians we have been given the proper armor and the weapons to rebuff the enemy and his kingdom's lies and attacks. He fights from a place of defeat, whereas we can fight from a place of victory.

"Therefore take up the whole armor of God, that you may be able to withstand in the evil day, and having done all, to stand firm. Stand therefore, having fastened on the belt of truth, and having put on the breastplate of righteousness, and, as shoes for your feet, having put on the readiness given by the gospel of peace. In all circumstances take up the shield of faith, with which you can extinguish all the flaming darts of the evil one; and take the helmet of salvation, and the sword of the Spirit, which is the word of God, praying at all times in the Spirit, with all prayer and supplication. To that end, keep alert with all perseverance, making supplication for all the saints, and also for me, that words may be given to me in opening my mouth boldly to proclaim the mystery of the gospel, for which I am an ambassador in chains, that I may declare it boldly, as I ought to speak."

EPHESIANS 6:13-20

Often, if I find myself in a bout of anxiety, I first recognize it for what it is, and second, try to think about where I am at in life. Interestingly, I will find myself feeling the most attacked either before, after, or while I am making some form of an impact in someone's life for the sake of the Gospel. During one week I remember clearly, a few years ago, I really could not figure out the root of the anxious attacks I was experiencing. I often find them being a result of my own disorganization—getting little to no sleep, staring at a screen for endless hours, drinking excessive amounts of caffeine even when I fully know it gives me jitters—but that week I could not quite put my finger on it. Not until one evening later in the week did my friend call me in the middle of a personal crisis seeking counsel. I was exhausted from having dealt with a hectic week and so nervous about saying the right words, but during that phone call I felt as if the Holy Spirit were simply using me as a messenger as He whispered words to me in my spirit and they simply flowed out of my mouth.

Scripture, words of encouragement, and just an overall presence of peaceful came out on the phone that evening by way of none other than the Spirit. The experience was encouraging not only for her but for me as well. That night, I was able to look back and see how the anxiety attacks could have been a result of the enemy feeling threatened that I would speak life into my friend, which I in fact ended up doing. He was trying to stop me, but the power of Christ led me directly to the task He had prepared for me to be used as His vessel. To be honest, that bout of anxiety did not really become a dark memory after all, but more of a hopeful moment to look back on. I understood that, through Christ, I was actually a threat to the kingdom of darkness. Please do not think that I am encouraging you to start welcoming spiritual attacks in; rather, I want you to have an understanding that when they arrive, you may find it helpful to change your perspective and see it as an opportunity to whoop the enemy's butt.

GOD-EMPOWERMENT RATHER
THAN SELF-EMPOWERMENT

We are living in an age in which self-empowerment is sought and celebrated, where we are called by culture to follow our hearts and act for ourselves. That all sounds great, until we find ourselves following our fleshly desires to places of darkness. Let me tell you: nothing is more empowering than the Spirit of God working inside of you. You may experience similar hardship as you go about writing. I find it interesting that just about every Christian author I spoke with in the process of writing this book brought up the topic of spiritual warfare, sometimes without me even asking about it. That said, each person I was privileged to speak with has produced something inspiring. One in particular is writer Carolyn Fraiser. Fraiser has had her work published in various Christian magazines and newspapers. When I asked her the biggest difference between writing secular versus Christian content, she said, "You're writing for God. You're writing to promote the Gospel, to further His Kingdom. It's a calling that drives you forward. There's also a lot of spiritual warfare that can take place during the writing process, because the enemy definitely does not want God's message to get out."

Whenever Fraiser finds herself in the middle of a spiritual attack, she reminds herself of the calling God set on her heart. "First, we have to remember that you are working for a much higher purpose. We are not doing this for ourselves.

We are doing this for God. Secondly, whether we fail or not, we're reflecting him. We are getting his message across. We are representing him in this world. That drives me forward," Fraiser said.

Another important principle that Fraiser highlighted in our conversation was understanding that God can see the big picture of our projects. As humans, we are limited to only seeing what is right here in front of us. We can't even see or even begin to fathom the amazing things God is doing behind the scenes that will impact what is ahead. "It all comes down to God's timing. In writing for Christian publications, we must keep that in mind. As writers, we don't always see the bigger picture. God does," Frasier emphasized. "Sometimes we just go through steps, only seeing the little pieces of the process, but he sees the bigger picture. Keeping that in mind helps me get through those struggling times. Because it's not just us doing the work. It's who we are working for. We're writing for him, and that gives us purpose."

SHARED PERSECUTION

I remember sitting in my very first journalism class at Liberty University as my professor began to describe the attributes of a good journalist: bold, nosy, persistent, curious—the list went on. However, we spent quite some time on the word "tough-skinned" as I proceeded to have a quarter-life crisis, coming to the realization that this very word was about the complete opposite of who I am. In fact, if you look up Deanna Drogan in the dictionary, I am pretty sure you will find the word "tough-skinned" as an antonym. I have always been super sensitive and the kind of girl who takes everything *super* personally. I began to wonder that day if writing would even be the field for me. I saw this whole tough-skinned thing come into play as I began to actually start publishing my articles online. If I were to ever write about controversial topics, I was bound to receive comments like "you're stupid," or "you're ignorant," and other harsh words that would attack my character. Most of the times these remarks hurt, but I just had to move on and understand that not everyone is going to have the same opinion as me.

See, the truth is, not everyone is going to like your work—which is actually okay. God created each of us with different, unique personalities and interests, and that is just a fact of life. But as Christians, we must especially recognize the fact that because we are not of this world, the world is actually going to reject us in the same way it rejected Christ. If you are going to stand for truth on your writing platform, understand that those who are not in Christ, according to scripture, are deaf from hearing the truth. John 8:45 is Jesus speaking to His opponents and says: ***"If I am telling the truth, why don't you believe me? Whoever belongs to God hears what God says. The reason you do not hear is that you do not***

belong to God." Truth is not always going to get through to people, because scripture tells us that they cannot hear truth for what it is, which is a sad fact. However, you should not stop writing about it and should most definitely not be afraid of what people will think if you actually take a stand for truth in your work.

I wholeheartedly believe that standing for truth and risking "hurting feelings" is one of the greatest acts of love we can express. Think about Jesus. All that He did was in love, but He was not afraid to be offensive and bold. **He let His love for the people around Him surpass the fear that He may hurt their feelings. Love is sacrificing our own reputation for the sake of the people around us.** Would you rather misguide your brothers and sisters, leading them further from truth to keep a good reputation? Or would you rather risk your reputation to point them toward Christ? Hopefully someday we can all get to the point where we choose the latter. I am still working on that myself. Note that, as Christian writers, we are actually not representing our own reputations, but that of Christ. Yes, your name will end up on the cover of the book, but if you are writing it for the glory of God, then truly what other people think of us should not matter as much.

I absolutely love author and pastor Dr. Charles Stanley. My roommate and I would fall asleep to his podcasts every night our junior year of college. Though his congregation is made up of an age group a bit above us, I think we might just be his biggest fans. He holds so much wisdom. In his message "Persecuted,"[12] he speaks about us sharing in the sufferings of Christ. "Persecution for the believer is our opportunity to share in the sufferings of Christ," Stanley said. "What did He suffer? All kinds of abuse, all kinds of extreme words directed towards Him that were ungodly, and finally they killed Him, and He died and rose again. So, when you and I suffer, it says we are sharing in the sufferings of Christ." Stanley then goes on to read 1 Peter 4:12-13, which says, *"Dear friends, do not be surprised at the fiery ordeal that has come on you to test you, as though something strange were happening to you. But rejoice inasmuch as you participate in the sufferings of Christ, so that you may be overjoyed when his glory is revealed."* Persecution, whether through a hateful review or another form of damaging words, can actually be used as a test. It asks: are you willing to continue to remain content and stand for Christ despite the persecution you might endure?

Dr. Stanley challenges his congregation with a tough question as he continues on in his message. He asks them, "Would you rather be accepted by the world than pleasing to Jesus?

---

12 Persecuted--Dr. Charles Stanley," YouTube video, 49:01, "In Touch Ministries," Feb. 1, 2015. https://www.youtube.com/watch?v=kWgVo8LtNio&t=1970s

You can't be both." Someone will always have a problem with you. You cannot possibly please everyone, *especially* if you are representing Christ. Take it from me, someone who struggles with people-pleasing on a daily basis: I wear myself out constantly trying to avoid any form of conflict and yet, it is almost inevitable. If you are going to represent Christ to the world, especially on a higher platform, I wouldn't necessarily say that you need to develop tough skin. Tough skin can only go so far—eventually, words are going to hurt. We have talked about the power words hold already. The true key to enduring the persecution from the world we share with Christ is to keep our eyes focused on Him, trusting that "he will make [us] adequate for whatever [our] situation may be," Stanley says—also keeping an eternal mindset trusting that we will be rewarded in Heaven for our works.

It is not easy to hear people criticize something you have worked on for endless hours—a project you shed blood, sweat, and tears over. Sometimes other Christians aren't even going to like your work! But if you are being obedient to the divine calling God has placed in your heart and you are writing for Him, the opinion of man slowly becomes less important. Of course, you want your work to be good, and though ultimately you are writing for God's glory, your book is for your readers as well—serving God and, by doing so, serving your brothers and sisters. That said, when criticism and persecution come your way, fix your eyes completely on Christ, and I guarantee whatever comes your way, you will find the strength to remain content and press on.

LESSONS AND TEACHINGS

- The enemy does not like you, and he does not like God, therefore he does not like you serving God.
- Spiritual warfare is something we should be aware of; attacks often happen when the enemy feels threatened by you. You need to understand that, through Christ, you have dominance over the enemy's kingdom. Use the weapons that Christ gives us in His word to fight.
- Understand that, despite what hardship goes on throughout the writing process, Christ can see the big picture of your project and is working behind the scenes.
- When you take a stand for Christ on a public platform, you need to be prepared for persecution from the world, but understand that telling people truth they do not want to hear is better than lies they do want to hear.

Here is a quick prayer you can pray before the next time you sit down to journal, blog, or write:

Dear Lord,
You are strong and mighty. I thank you for the victory I have in your Son's death, burial, and resurrection. As I sit down to write today, I pray against all schemes and tactics of the enemy

that he wants to use to keep me from completing the task you have set before me, in Jesus' Name. I pray that you would help me press on and fix my eyes on you despite the hardships and possible persecution that come my way. Let my love for my readers outweigh my desire to protect my own reputation. Use me to share your truth to a broken world on this platform you have given me. In Jesus' Name I pray. Amen

CHAPTER 7

THE ROLE OF THE MESSENGER

———

"For the word of God is alive and active. Sharper than any double-edged sword, it penetrates even to dividing soul and spirit, joints and marrow; it judges the thoughts and attitudes of the heart."

HEBREWS 4:12

AN ALIVE AND ACTIVE WORD

I'll be completely honest with you for a second (might as well—by now you probably know more about me than you want to). Having grown up in the church, in Christian schools, Bible studies, chapels, youth groups, small groups, accountability groups, discipleship groups, Sunday schools—you know, basically every form of Christian gathering that exists for young people— I have at times actually come to the conclusion that I have learned just about everything there is to know about the Bible. That's right: in my own human ignorance and pride, I have actually had moments when I felt as though I did not *need* to read my Bible, because I already knew *everything* in it already. Now, I know God is in the background somewhere just holding in a chuckle, because every time I think an outrageous thought like that, He proves otherwise.

Maybe this feeling has happened to you too. Have you ever read or heard a Bible passage so many times, but then ten years down the road, you learn something completely new from it that you had never even thought about or known before? For example, I had read and learned about the temptation of Jesus so many times, especially with it being a big part of my testimony and battle against anxiety, but not until a few years ago did I notice something unique about it that changed my perspective. God brought to my attention that the scriptures actually say in verse 1 that ***"Jesus was led by the <u>Spirit</u> into the wilderness to be tempted by the devil."*** Immediately, I was puzzled.

Why would God be leading God into the desert to be tempted? Oh, yeah, that makes complete sense (said no one ever). But then I realized all this time I had been missing out on such a beautiful part of this story. Really, the Holy Spirit leads Jesus into the desert here for *our* sake. Hebrews 4:15 reads: ***"For we do not have a high priest who is unable to empathize with our weaknesses, but we have one who has been tempted in every way, just as we are—yet he did not sin."*** The Holy Spirit led Jesus into the desert so that He would be able to empathize with us when we experience temptation from the enemy, and not only that, but to show us a perfect example of how to ward off the enemy and his temptations.

So, how is it that no matter how many times we read these stories and passages, we continue to learn new things every time we open up our Bibles? Because God's word is alive and active. The words we write have the potential to be powerful. I mean, how amazing is the thought that the very words God places in your heart could potentially change someone else's life? I have read some powerful books, some powerful blogs, some powerful poems, but only one book I know of is actually alive and active. Wow. How often do we actually sit and process that? The Bible is not simply a book filled with words; it's so much more than that.

Though written with the hand of man, 2 Timothy tells us that scripture was actually *breathed* out by God. While I fully believe that God is inspiring writers every single day, giving them words filled with power, no book will ever hold the same life-transforming power as the Bible. God's word is the ultimate, inerrant authority and the most definitive source of truth. Scripture tells us that God's word is actually a weapon—sharper than any double-edged sword. This weapon has come in handy several times throughout hardships I have faced, particularly my testimony and victory over anxiety, but also whenever I am faced with lies that tell me I am not good enough or will never measure up. In those times, I can look to God's word and combat deceit with the truth.

THE WORD AS OUR MODEL

We cannot expect to write a book as powerful as the Bible, but we can use our books to *further* the truth of that word. That said, as Christian authors we must fill ourselves with the word of God so that what we write is grounded in His truths and therefore filled with power. If our goal in our writing is to deepen our readers' relationships with Jesus, we need to incorporate principles from His very word into our commentary. We must also use the Bible as a model for how we should go about writing. The authors of each book of the Bible divinely wrote down the words God was telling them to write. They had no power to write life-transforming content on their own; they were simply the messengers of God's love letters to His people.

Jason Benham took the time to share with me some of the importance of grounding your work in God's word. "We should all study the Scriptures to 'show ourselves approved,' as the verse says. We don't just read it, but diligently dig for deep truths to apply to our own life," Benham said. The verse he referred to is 2 Timothy 2:15, which reads, *"Do your best to present yourself to God as one approved, a worker who has no need to be ashamed, rightly handling the word of truth."* "In a writing project, the truths you have studied and applied for yourself will come back to you at just the right moment to add to your stories," Benham said. To be honest, I never really fully understood what 2 Timothy 2:15 meant.

Does it mean we need to prove ourselves to God? Does it mean we are to work to gain His approval and His favor? No. God loves us despite ourselves—despite our sinfulness, shortcomings, and imperfections. We should present ourselves to God as one approved, not out of obligation to *gain* approval, but out of our authentic love for Him and desire to stand before Him unashamed. If we truly love God with all our hearts, souls, and minds, we should do everything in our power to please Him and obey His commands. Don't you want to please your Father? Don't you look forward to the day you stand before Him, gazing into His precious face as He says, "Well done"? If we want to speak these words, we must be rightly handling His truths, not just by reading them, but by actually applying them into our own lives.

Sorry, I started preaching for a second. Back to Jason.

"Writing is timeless. When we read Scripture, we're literally reading the words of a man who wrote them thousands of years ago. It's like he's talking to us as we read his words. Now, with the Bible we know it was divinely inspired so God is the One speaking to us. But our writing is much the same—we gain inspiration from God and then write so that the reader will hear directly from Him," Benham explained. "When you have this perspective then you know no matter how good the book is, you were simply the messenger."

Wow, if that is not a piece of encouragement for an aspiring writer today, I don't know what is. What an honor it is to have the opportunity imitate the writers of the Bible in our own work. We get to listen to what God has to say to us and be the messengers of His words, much similarly to the authors of scripture. The thought of sharing the truth of Christ with our audience should excite us far more than the success of our work. What makes a good Christian book is not the number of copies sold, but the willingness of the author to implement content that God wants him or her to share. The idea of even just one life being changed by the words God should give us the motivation to press on. Being a Christian writer is a unique opportunity; it is a chance to actually be the messengers of Christ to people who need to hear what He has to say to them, similarly structured to how the authors of each book of the Bible took God's words and scribed the greatest story ever told.

A TWO-WAY CONVERSATION

Jeremiah 33:3 reads, *"Call to me and I will answer you and tell you great and unsearchable things you do not know."* This verse is a prayer, and I think if we actually understood the impact of our prayers, we would find ourselves setting aside more time for it on a day-to day basis—I am speaking to myself here. When we pray, we are actually entering into the Heavenly realms: the perfect place to speak to our Father, but more importantly to hear from Him. I think a common misconception surrounding prayer suggests that it is simply a one-way conversation—a time in which we read out our requests to God like a grocery list, in hopes that someday He will go in and fix them somewhere far off in the distance. Jeremiah tells us that when we call out to God, *He will answer us and tell us great unsearchable things that we do not know.*

I don't know about you, but I want to learn new things from God. I want to hear the great things that He has to share with me, because I first and foremost want to know Him better, and because I want Him to show me how to live a life abundantly. We are living in a sad time where so many believe that God no longer speaks to His children, that his doing so was something only done in "biblical times." I can tell you firsthand that is a lie straight from the enemy, who does not want to see lives changed from the things God has to tell us. The same God who spoke to His people throughout the scriptures has not changed and is still speaking to His people today. We are the ones who need to make sure we are attentive and listening.

Reverend Jerry Falwell once said, "Nothing of eternal value is ever accomplished apart from prayer." *Can you tell I went to Liberty University yet?* As Christian writers, if we want our work to be of eternal value, our books should be centered around prayer, but we need to recognize that prayer does not just look like us calling out to God asking that He would help us write a good book. It looks like us calling out to God and asking Him how He can work in us to write a good book—then, of course, taking the time to listen and apply what He has to say. Author Lisa Whittle said that she cannot even imagine writing anything without prayer. "Well, I mean, I say that I tried to write things without prayer. I've tried to just dive into my own talents, and just start writing something; it just doesn't work. Prayer is a huge part of the process. And it's not just like a quick prayer—you know, *God, give me something to write about.* At least for me, it's been this sort of an ongoing dialogue I've had with the Lord, where he's showing things in my life. And the next thing I know, eight months later, I realize he's been showing me things for a book."

Here is a perfectly clear image of Jeremiah 3:33 right here. I love how Whittle actually calls prayer an ongoing dialogue. Do not get me wrong: there is a way to pray and a way not to, in a sense. Jesus says, *"And when you pray, do not be like the hypocrites, for they love to pray standing in the synagogues and on the street corners to be seen by others. Truly I tell you, they have received their reward in full. But when you pray, go into your room, close the door and pray to your Father, who is unseen. Then your Father, who sees what is done in secret, will reward you. And when you pray, do not keep on babbling like pagans, for they think they will be heard because of their many words. Do not be like them, for your Father knows what you need before you ask him."*

What I love about this passage is that shows Jesus simply looking for one thing from us when we pray: our hearts. If we are praying to seek the approval of others, our hearts are evidently not quite in the right place during that moment. Jesus wants to hear from the real, raw, authentic *you*, not some rehearsed, made-up version of yourself. I think we have developed this stigma that the only way we can pray is to formally close our eyes, bow our heads, and speak this beautiful-sounding song to the Lord, filled with tons of "thous" and "shalls." That is not the case. Prayer could look like you driving in the car down a beautiful road just expressing to the Lord your thankfulness—hopefully your eyes would not be closed then. Prayer could be you snuggled up on the couch at sunrise with some tea, sitting in silence before the Lord, asking Him to speak. It could look like the random moments throughout the day when you need His guidance and direction and seek Him in the most random of places. Oh, and if you like to write—which I am assuming you do at least a little bit if you are reading this—maybe try out writing in a prayer journal.

"It's not like, you know, I intended on writing a book or got into it going, *Hey God, I hope you'll help me by giving me some kind of title or whatever.* It's really been us just dialoguing about something that needed to change, usually in me. And then, after all of that, me realizing, *Oh, this is something you want me to share with other people, too?*" Whittle said.

Writing a book might be an amazing opportunity for you to strengthen your prayer life, so don't waste it. Use it as an opportunity to press into Jesus more than you ever have before. Maybe you have never had an ongoing dialogue with the Lord. Maybe you have always thought prayer was only something done as the pastor asks the congregation to close their eyes and bow their heads. Prayer can be so much more than that. It is a two-way conversation in which we should be expectant that the Lord is going to speak to us. Don't be afraid to ask Him specific questions, because He loves to hear from His children and He delights in sharing amazing things with them. Who knows—maybe what He shares with you will become what He wants you to share with others.

LESSONS AND TEACHINGS

- You can never learn all there is to know about the Bible because God's word is alive and active and always moving hearts.
- Though our content will never hold the same amount of power that the Bible does, we can use it as a model and perfect example of divine inspiration.
- Your projects should be surrounded by prayer.
- Despite the common stigmas around prayer, it truly is a two-way conversation, not just a one-sided conversation. When we take time to listen to what God has to share with us in prayer, we can not only learn from Him but also implement His words into our writing to impact others.

Here is a quick prayer you can pray before the next time you sit down to journal, blog, or write:

Dear Lord,
I thank you so much for your word and the fact that it is alive and active. When I open it up, I pray that your Holy Spirit would reveal to me new things that I have never learned before. I ask that you would fill me up with your wisdom, so that

it will pour it out into my work, making it centered around your truths. I also ask that you would strengthen my prayer life and remind me that it is a two-way conversation. Let me make more time to be still and listen the wonderful things you have to share with me. I pray that my work would always be centered around your word and around the things you share with me in prayer. In Jesus' Name I pray, Amen

CHAPTER 8

SURROUNDING YOURSELF WITH THE BODY

———

*"As iron sharpens iron, so one
person sharpens another."*

PROVERBS 27:17

SETTING YOURSELF UP FOR CREATIVE SUCCESS

I believe I am one of those equally extroverted and introverted type of people.

Don't get me wrong: I am most definitely not the loudest person in a room, and I sure do adore my fair share of alone time in a comfortable space—particularly one close to a TV and a container of ice cream—but too much time alone makes me almost a bit stir crazy. I love to be around people, even if that just means sitting in the same room in silence together. I recall one time I had a huge writing assignment due at midnight, but my roommates and group of friends were downstairs giggling at one of my favorite chick flicks. The FOMO (fear of missing out) was killing me as I sat upstairs in my room/dungeon, stuck trying to get past the part of the paper where you write your name and date. *That's it*, I thought as I slammed my computer shut and carried it down the stairs to finish up the assignment as I quoted the rest of *She's the Man* and spent the night giggling along with my friends. Did that assignment turn out well? Sure, but it was most definitely not my best work, due to my relative lack of focus.

I fully believe that everyone has his or her own work style. For me, when I *actually* want to get stuff done, I love venturing off to my favorite cozy smoothie bowl shop with twinkly lights and turning on my beloved French gypsy jazz Spotify playlist. But the key for me to actually get things done is that I must discipline myself by limiting all distractions—especially people. This may just be my opinion, but I believe that writing or truly any type of creative activity involves a certain level of focus that differs from any other type of work, I guess because creative work involves so much inspiration. See, as writers, our work differs a lot from the average nine-to-five office job. We are usually free to work wherever we want, at any hour we want—which is a pretty great thing, if you ask me. However, with writing a book, it's not like you arrive at work and say hi to the sweet lady at the front desk and engage in team meetings throughout the day. Writing or really any type of freelance position can become an isolating activity. If you are extroverted like me, as a writer you might end up lacking in that community aspect you crave. Even if you are more introverted, we were all designed for community.

COMMUNAL GOD, COMMUNAL PEOPLE

Think about God. He is a trinity—each person of the Godhead: the Father, the Son and the Holy Spirit is in communion with the other. I used to be so confused in Genesis when God would refer to Himself using the term "us." Genesis 1:26 reads, *"Then God said, 'Let us make man in our image, in our likeness, and let them rule over the fish of the sea and the birds of the air, over the livestock, over all the earth, and over all the creatures that move along the ground."* Like, okay, God, who else was there with you that day—am I missing something? Hello, news flash, He is talking about the trinity here! A trinity that works in perfect harmony, unity, and communion with each other. Because we are made in God's image—we were also made for community. Proverbs tells us that as iron sharpens iron, a person sharpens a person, which is why it is so important not just as writers but as Christian that we ensure we are surrounding ourselves with Godly people, who will point us toward Christ.

Fiction Christian author Francine Rivers writes in an article titled "Writing Tips"[13] on her website, FrancineRivers.com: "Don't allow your writing to isolate and insulate you. We can't write about all kinds of people and views realistically if we close ourselves off from people. Remember, too, that you aren't just in church to feed your soul. You are there to encourage others. They need you as much as you need them."

So, as people susceptible to isolation, we must make sure we are taking time to be poured into by others. Hopefully you are plugged into a church community and involved there, but you can find other ways to expand your involvement in a community, such as:

1. **Attending a Bible study.**
2. **Meeting with an accountability group.**
3. **Taking breaks throughout the week to meet a good friend for coffee.**

---

13   Rivers, Francine. "Writing Tips". Francine Rivers. https://francine-rivers.com/writing-tips/ (October 10, 2019).

Whatever community may look like for you, be sure that you are taking this special time to connect with others, because the truth is that people are inspiring, and they have amazing stories to tell. You really never know who you are going to learn from. You might even find yourself using other people's stories to further the message of your book (with their permission, of course).

THE IMPORTANCE OF ROUTINE COMMUNITY

In college, I lived on campus in a dorm for three years and then off campus in a town house for my senior year. My junior year, I served on hall leadership, and we were required to be part of an accountability group with fellow leaders on our team. I remember wondering how in the world I was going to balance eighteen credits on top of making time to pour my heart out weekly to five strangers, but little did I know that meeting with this group of girls would completely change my life. For one, I fully believe that sharing what is going on in your life with others is healthy. Holding that all in every day is unhealthy. Journaling can be very good for this, but actually sharing face to face with people who care about you and might have words of encouragement is vital.

Week after week, at each meeting, whether in a dorm room, at a coffee shop, or in the dining hall, I would find myself feeling relieved and refreshed as I summoned the courage to open up and share how my week was going. I'm not just talking the whole surface-level, typical college student, *I'm drowning in homework, only eating Ramen noodles, hardly sleeping* kind of thing. We would get deep. These girls ended up knowing about my deepest insecurities and struggles and what was so beautiful about that is we created an environment in which I felt comfortable and welcomed to share. I noticed a big difference that year compared to the next when I moved off campus. Yes, I had friends I felt I could talk to at any given moment, but it was not the same as having that consistent, healthy time dedicated to accountability and community with others. When engaged in consistent accountability, I found myself a little bit more joyful than normal, feeling a bit more free and at rest knowing I always had someone who would listen to me, and I to them.

The beauty of community is also that you never know what impact you are going to have on those you spend time with. Not to toot my own horn, but only to point back at God's brilliance, sometimes in that group, words I gave to the girls encouraged them. Sharing our struggles, the things we have buried deep down in the dark, can often be a light in other people's lives. Of course, not by the mere fact that you are struggling, but by their understanding that they are finally not alone and can walk alongside you and wrestle that common struggle together. Community is vital no matter what your vocation might be. But because writing has the power to cause isolation, you have to prioritize time to spend in fellowship with others.

LESSONS AND TEACHINGS

- Creative work takes a different level of focus; do your best to make your writing environment one with limited distractions.
- Being a writer or a freelance creator differs from your average nine-to-five job. It is easy to become isolated and lack that crucial aspect of community.
- We were designed in God's image and He is a trinity, meaning He is communal.
- Being in community with each other allows us to inspire others, and them to inspire us. People have amazing stories and we can learn from each other in ways we don't even realize.

Here is a quick prayer you can pray before the next time you sit down to journal, blog, or write:

Dear Lord,
Thank you that I am made in your image and that you are a creator. I pray for the supernatural ability to focus as I sit down to write about you. Calm my mind and my thoughts and create an atmosphere of peace around me as I work, so that I can press in and hear what you have to share with me. I pray

that despite the need for limited distractions while I work, that outside of my work you would provide me with a community of believers who challenge me to be the best version of myself. In Jesus' Name I pray, Amen

CHAPTER 9

REACHING UNBELIEVERS

———

"I am astonished that you are so quickly deserting
him who called you in the grace of Christ and
are turning to a different gospel— not that there
is another one, but there are some who trouble
you and want to distort the gospel of Christ."

GALATIANS 1:6-7

MISREPRESENTING LOVE

Recently, at church, our pastor presented us with a question that needed to be addressed: "With a show of hands," he began, "how many of you at some point have been hurt by the church?" Sadly, I cannot recall one hand not being raised, and I think that was really the point of his message. First off, I must say that unfortunately, being hurt by people in the church is inevitable, because the church is made up of people, and people are far from perfect. If you haven't figured that out yet, I personally would like to hang out with your friends and family. Second, I fully believe we are living in a broken time, in which members of the church are falsely representing the love of Christ in day-to-day interactions, often turning unbelievers away from the church. As Christian authors, our ultimate goal through our writing should be to bring our readers closer to the Lord, but how do we go about doing that for unbelievers? Reaching unbelievers can often be a challenging task—especially if we are relying on our human power to do so. Thankfully, we serve a God who works through us to draw others to Himself. But how do we go about reaching those who have been hurt by the church and want nothing to do with it? How do we go about spreading the greatest story ever told to the ones who have done everything they can possibly do to run far from it?

I remember scrolling through Facebook recently to come across a post about a robbery that happened down the road from my house at our local fruit stand. The post featured a surveillance video that captured two young men breaking into the cash register, and a status asking if anyone recognized them. Thousands of people had commented on it, and being the nosy person I am, I sought to know more about the situation, so I began to read the comments. I read one comment that said something along the lines of "praying for this situation and all involved." Directly under that was another comment from a different woman who wrote, "I won't be praying because praying does nothing." At first, in my human flesh of course, I could not help but take offense to that as I continued to sit there thinking, *How could she say such a thing? Who does this lady think she is?* Then the Holy Spirit gently turned my offense into a strong compassion.

Ok, so you may be thinking, *Man, she has way too much time on her hands to get caught up 300 comments down in a Facebook post about a robbery at a local fruit stand*, but God in His brilliance of course actually brought something very serious to my attention that day. I saw people replying to this woman's comment saying mean things like "you are crazy, lady, prayer works," or "you need Jesus, you psycho." I may have been reading into things a bit too much, but I could not help but pause and think: *Here is a woman who has probably walked through something very challenging in her life and prayed about it only to see the situation remain or get worse.* Haven't we all been through this before? I sure know I have. And here we have people claiming to represent Christ, yet missing out on the greatest commandment: love. Because God is love, according to 1 John 4:8; we are to be bearers of this love, showing others the gentle, compassionate character of Christ. Somewhere along the line, the church became judgment-bearers, people with some absurd, egotistic belief that we are so great that we actually have a right to place judgment on our brother or sister, when in reality the Gospel says that none is good except Christ. We have turned the Gospel into a message that is not a welcoming invitation but more of a standard others are to reach. We claim to represent one thing, but proclaim the exact opposite, only leading people further away—and I put we in there because I can be guilty of this failing too.

REACHING THOSE WHO HAVE BEEN HURT BY THE CHURCH

Although I have so many tips and insights to share with those writing for a Christian audience to strengthen their faith, what about writing for those who do not believe? First off, thank you for your desire to fulfill the Great Commission— we are *all* called to make disciples and share Christ with those who do not know Him. Secondly, how exactly are you supposed to write to these people, particularly those who have been so hurt by the church and want nothing to do with the message of Jesus that has sadly become distorted to them? Christian author Kristen Billerbeck, also known as the "Queen of Chick Lit," used to be one of these people. Now a bestselling author whose work has been featured in the New York Times and on "The Today Show," Billerbeck says her work is "not secular enough for the secular market and not Christian enough for the Christian market." Billerbeck grew up in a Catholic home and did not become a Christian until she was twenty-four. "Christians stood in the way of me and Jesus," Billerbeck said.

What a scary thought—the people whose mission should be to steer others toward Christ being the very obstacle keeping them from Him. "I just did not like the way people who were calling themselves Christians were acting," Billerbeck said. "It was very judgmental, and very cold, and I did not want to be like that. So, I did not want to be a Christian."

Knowing what it is like to be on the outside has given Billerbeck a unique perspective when sharing the message of Christ in her books. "I think my platform has really been to talk to the people who are outside and talk to the people who are inside and say, 'Don't ruin it for these people,'" Billerbeck said. Billerbeck's work has been said by one of her readers to be like "deep truths that are embedded in milk chocolate." She uses her fiction and light-hearted style to subtly drop impactful truths to her readers. "I really want a fun message; I want people to read a story that they get enthralled with, and come away thinking about it. I want to get those truths out there, but I don't want people to know they're getting a message," Billerbeck said.

The other day I sat at a car place to get an oil change. I brought my laptop and my textbooks because I knew I would be sitting there for a while staring at the wall in front of me. But the day started to get interesting when a customer and an employee at the front desk started to get into a deep conversation. The customer asked the employee about his thoughts on Christianity. I peeked from behind my laptop, trying not to look as though I were being nosy—though I totally was. The employee looked as though he wanted to be anywhere except there but was respectful enough to continue in a dialogue with this customer. Though he spoke softly, I can still hear his response in my head: "I am just sick of having Christians shove the Gospel down my throat." *Ouch.* That just broke my heart.

Taking a similar approach to Billerbeck's technique might be helpful when writing to an audience of people who have been hurt by the church. "I think that's a good base for any Christian author to have, because you want to get these truths across, but you don't want your reader to feel like they've been sold by it," Billerbeck said. I am not here to tell you how to write the book or work God is calling you to, and Billerbeck isn't either. I am fully convinced that if you ask God to help you write something that will impact a crowd that has been hurt by the church, He will show you the proper way of doing so. That said, I think often you will find God guiding you to write something *for* your crowd rather than at them. Remember before your fingers hit the keyboard or your pen touches the paper who you are representing in your work—a loving, gentle God who is quick to welcome anyone into His family.

REPRESENTING CHRIST OUTSIDE OF OUR WORK

If we are messengers for Christ, we must represent Him not only in our work, but outside of it as well. A good writer actually believes in the words he or she writes and lives by them—though hopefully not if you write horror. Scripture tells us to not only talk the talk, but to walk the walk. For instance, James 1:20-23 says, *"But be doers of the word, and not hearers only, deceiving yourselves. For if anyone is a hearer of the word and not a doer, he is like a man who looks intently at his natural face in a mirror."* We have talked a lot about authenticity throughout this book, which is one of the most crucial aspects of writing something impactful. Pointing out a hypocrite isn't hard. I immediately think of the Pharisees. They claimed to be these ultra-spiritual leaders, yet they completely rejected the Savior and treated Him with disrespect. In Matthew 23, Jesus calls them out for their hypocrisy: *"Woe to you, teachers of the law and Pharisees, you hypocrites! You shut the door of the kingdom of heaven in people's faces. You yourselves do not enter, nor will you let those enter who are trying to."*

First off, side note: can we talk about how cool Jesus is? Yes, He was gentle, but He also knew how to boldly stand up for truth, something I wish I had more courage to do. If we are representing Christ in our books and using our platforms as Christian authors to lead our readers closer to Christ, we must ensure we are leading Godly lives in our every day. You can't possibly be instructing your readers to love their brother or sister while treating the people around you like they do not matter. Well, I guess you could, but that is dangerous ground to tread. Hypocrisy itself is so dangerous, especially in a position where you are leading or influencing other, because it can have the power to cause confusion and possibly even lead others astray. I don't know about you, but I don't think I would want anything to do with God if someone supposedly representing His love treated me with a harsh spirit of judgment—a completely false representation of everything God is.

In today's day and age, hypocrisy has become so easy, especially by means of social media. You see people at church or small group one day, and the next watch an Instagram story of them trying to keep their balance after a drink too many. What does that say to someone interested in getting to know the person of Christ? Now, a disclaimer before I go any further: Christ does not expect your perfection. If He did, why would He have chosen to die on the cross and shower us in His grace? But we must do our absolute best to represent Him and His word in all that we say and do, especially if He gives us a higher platform to represent Him. We have all heard the message a million times: be careful what you put out on the internet because what is deleted never truly is deleted. That mantra may be cliche, but it is crucial. Today people can dig up your information at the snap of a finger. Take it from my friends who see an eligible guy and the next second are telling me his relationship status and his blood type. Social media can be an excellent tool for marketing your book and your brand as a content creator, but make sure that your brand is glorifying to Christ.

LESSONS AND TEACHINGS

- Somewhere along the line, the church has turned the welcoming Gospel of Jesus into a standard that unbelievers must reach.
- If we are not treating our brothers and sisters with the love of Christ, then we are misrepresenting everything He is.
- Writing for an audience of unbelievers and people who may have been hurt by the church can be done in a way that is not overbearing but rather subtly impactful.
- We as Christian authors have to represent Christ in our work and outside of it. We can't just walk the walk, but must also talk the talk.

Here is a quick prayer you can pray before the next time you sit down to journal, blog, or write:

Dear Lord,

I thank you that you are a God of love. I ask that you would help me show that love to my brothers and sisters around me. Lord, I also pray that you would just make it very clear to me as to whom you would like my audience to be for this project. God, if it's believers, I pray that you would let this content strengthen their faith in you. If it is nonbelievers, I pray that you would soften their hearts and open their ears to what you have to share with them, and ultimately lead them to you. In Jesus' Name I pray,

Amen.

CHAPTER 10

IN THE END, KNOWING YOUR IDENTITY IS NOT ON THE FRONT COVER

"I have been crucified with Christ. It is no longer I who live, but Christ who lives in me. And the life I now live in the flesh I live by faith in the Son of God, who loved me and gave himself for me."

GALATIANS 2:20

THE SEARCH FOR SELF

Unfortunately, we are living in a time when people define us by the clothes we wear, the job we hold, the people we talk to, the places we go—the list could go on forever. In a culture set up that way, it is easy to fall into the trap of believing maybe that is the truth. I went through an odd period of longing during my first couple years of college. I remember meeting with my accountability partner at Starbucks and looking her in the eye across the table telling her, "I feel like I am just still trying to figure out who I am." She looked a bit puzzled at me as those words came out of my mouth. "What do you mean?" she asked. To be honest, I didn't really know what I meant either.

This season of life led to a lot of anxiety and pressure. I was constantly wracking my brain trying to figure out who in the world I was and what my purpose was going to be. The worst part of it all was that I felt like everyone else had it all figured out. Was I the funny girl who would only crack my best jokes to the ones I felt most comfortable around, or was I maybe more of the approachable, serious, down-to-earth kinda girl? Was I the aspiring, nosy journalist like an Andie Anderson from *How to Lose a Guy in 10 Days* or more of an Andy Sachs from *The Devil Wears Prada*: timid, but hardworking? (If you can't tell, I sort of have a thing for chick-flicks.) We often say in the Christian community that we are to find our identities in Christ. Trying to look "ultra-spiritual," I used to pretend I knew what that meant. In small groups or accountability groups, when I was asked what I was working on in my life, that was always my go-to answer: "Oh, ya know, I'm just really working to find my identity in Christ, that's all." Hello, news flash, finding your identity is a *big deal*, sort of a life-changer—and there I was, casually throwing it around in conversation.

One late night, as I was attempting to fall asleep cozied up in my bed with my favorite thieves essential oil flowing through my diffuser, listening to one of my favorite podcasts, "Set Apart Girl," I shot up in the dark, with the moon as my only source of light, in realization. Author and founder of the podcast Leslie Ludy was speaking in her episode titled "Discovering Your True Identity"[14] about how to truly find out who we really are—a question I was trying to discover the answer to. She said, "I constantly heard this message of, 'Tap into your true self. Learn who you really are. Express yourself to the world!' But I didn't know how to do that. I didn't know who I was," Ludy said. "So I began to feel like, *Do I even have value and worth because I can't figure out what this unique thing about me is or what my 'true self' really is?* And then I began to realize that I was looking to the wrong source to define who I was. I was looking to myself instead of Jesus, and that was such a refreshing wake-up call for me."

As soon as she spoke those words, I knew I would not be getting any more sleep that night; I went from being snuggled up

---

14 Ludy, Leslie. "Discovering Your True Identity." *Set Apart Girl*. Podcast audio, Oct. 15, 2017.

to sitting on the edge of my bed in eagerness. Every word she spoke was so relatable and showed me that maybe I was not alone in this constant search for self. That night, I realized that the reason I was having such a hard time defining my own self was because I, in my own humanity, do not even have that capability: it is God who defines me. See, I came to realize that night that my identity is not the stuff I have, nor the things I do, the people I make laugh, or even the people I don't—it is actually Jesus Christ Himself. I think we are all on this ongoing search for self. We try to find ourselves in our talents, whether they be music, sports, or writing. These skills are often blessings but will never lead us to the most true and satisfying answer. I love, love, *love* this quote that Ludy used from Christian author Elisabeth Elliot :"The world looks for happiness through self-assertion. The Christian knows that joy is found in self-abandonment. 'If a man will let himself be lost for My sake,' Jesus said, 'he will find his true self.'"

IDENTITY IN CHRIST, NOT WORK

So, how does this tie into authoring a Christian book, you might ask? Well, I have to believe that your identity in Christ ties into just about every aspect of your life—only highlighting the importance of it once again. Seeing your name on the cover of a book is an exciting moment, looking back, thinking, *Wow, I did that.* Publishing a book is truly an amazing accomplishment, and telling the people around you that you are a published author is certainly kind of cool, but what about the times your book tanks, or you receive negative feedback? What about when the best work you put out there ends up costing you boatloads more than the amount that you make from it? Such outcomes hurt and are not very fun.

Though you should absolutely love what you are doing—you should introduce yourself as an author and get excited seeing your name on a front cover after long nights of hard work—you need to remember that you are not defined by your work. Your identity is not in the name on the front cover of your book, the success of your book, or its failure; it is in none other than Jesus Christ. Galatians 2:20 says that *"if we have been crucified with Christ, it is no longer [we] who lives, but Him"*—meaning we lost our lives to pick up His. We no longer need to search for our own self-worth because our worth is not only in Christ, but it actually is Christ! Ludy said, "As, you put self aside, as you stop focusing on self, and as you start focusing on Him and saying, 'Lord, I want all selfish things to be pushed aside, to get out of the way, to be denied, and I want to become a vessel for You to work through, to shine Your light and Your glory to this world,' that's when you'll find your true identity. If your goal in every conversation, every decision and action that you do is to point eyes back to Jesus Christ, then you know that you're walking in God's true purpose for your life."

What a beautiful place to be—walking in Christ's true purpose for your life. Now, you can take a deep breath and release that load of unease and unnecessary baggage you have been carrying that was only meant for Christ to bear. Relax and enjoy the process of writing your book, understanding that no matter what happens with it your identity is in Christ.

OUTRO

Well, friend, can I just say what an absolute pleasure it has been? I want to thank you for inviting me into your reading time. Thank you for bearing with my several off-topic rabbit trails and moments of absolute silliness. I mean, without them I don't really think you would have gotten to know me. Now, here is where I bring up my final point, and that is to simply be yourself in your writing. Be the authentic, goofy, imperfect you that God made you to be. I can't say much than that. Christ made you who you are for a reason. With a fresh knowledge that He is your ultimate identity, understand that you are free to express the unique person He designed you to be through your content creation. The truth is that there is only one you. Your writing voice differs from the next authors. Comparing your voice to another will never leave you satisfied.

I am fully aware that my writing voice differs immensely from that of C.S. Lewis. Yeah, that stinks in a way, because he is probably one of the most well-known, profound Christian authors to walk the Earth. But he is not me, and I am not him. I admire many Christian authors, including all of those mentioned in this book, and I look to their work as a model of what good Christian books should look like. But, if I find myself trying to mimic their exact writing styles, I most likely will restrict myself in a way. I think we all have this idea that processes like writing a book or producing music or painting a picture all have to look a particular way and if we break one of the fundamental rules, the result will be a complete disaster, but the beauty of creative work is that it really does not have to always look a certain way. What looked one way for C.S. Lewis might look completely different for me.

Really, that principle is important for life. We hear "stay in your lane" all the time, but what does that really mean? I've gathered that it means understanding your life is not limited to a box. Here I am, sitting on my family's porch, a few months into life as a college graduate, applying for several jobs, only to have heard nothing back yet. I always thought that life worked in one way: you go to college and graduate, and then you get married or go straight into a job. Here I am doing neither of those things as I see post after post about new adventures, engagements, and positions of fellow friends and classmates. It can be hard from time to time, but who says my life is supposed to look a certain way? Is there some hidden rule book out there suggesting that if one rule is broken, my life suddenly doesn't matter anymore? The truth is: we serve an exciting, adventurous, and unexpected kind of God. One who writes His own exciting stories personal to each of His children. Every version is going to look different, and that is beautiful.

So, as you embark on this writing journey, I hope you take into consideration some of what I have learned from some amazing, experienced authors, and what I felt God placed in my heart to share. But remember that the book-writing path God has set before you might look different than mine. The most important part is putting yourself in a position from which you are able to hear from Him, learn from Him, and experience a communion with Him that you might not have ever experienced before. He will guide you in the process and make it one worthwhile. My heart in this book is not only that you have learned helpful principles of good writing, but really principles to apply to your life and your walk with Christ. Live for His glory, be used as His vessel, don't be afraid to share your story with others, speak words of encouragement to your brothers and sisters, lay yourself down and learn to surrender, fight the invisible fight with the tools at hand, seek to be Christ's messenger in all you do, make an external impact in the way you treat people, and most importantly, understand that your identity is found in none other than Christ Himself.

Now go make an impact. The world needs your light.

APPENDIX

INTRODUCTION

1. Dietrich, William. "The Writer's Odds of Success." *Huff-Post*, May 4, 2013. https://www.huffpost.com/entry/the-writers-odds-of-succe_b_2806611 (Oct.10, 2019)

CHAPTER 1:

1. Piper, John. "Has God Called Me to Write?" Desiring God. https://www.desiringgod.org/ (Oct.10, 2019).
2. "Sub-creation." Tolkien Gateway. http://tolkiengateway. net/wiki/Sub-creation (Oct. 10, 2019).
3. Whittle, Lisa. "Author." Lisa Whittle. https://lisawhittle. com/ (Oct. 10, 2019).

CHAPTER 2:

1. "Benham, Jason and David. "Are You Ready to Live Powerfully?" Whatever the Cost | Benham Brothers. https://whateverthecost.com/ (Oct. 10, 2019).

CHAPTER 3:

1. Jeffers, Qené Manon. *A Peace Unfettered: My Anthology of Faith.* WestBow Press, 2018.
2. Putnam, John. *He Spends, She Spends: Why God Wants You to Live For Free.* Fedd Books, 2016.

CHAPTER 4:

1. Hickory, Jonathan. *Break Every Chain: A Police Officer's Battle with Alcoholism, Depression, and Devastating Loss; And the True Story of How God Changed His Life Forever.* Covenant Books, 2018.
2. Lucado, Max. "The Write Stuff." MaxLucado.com https://maxlucado.com/writing-corner-tips-tools-aspiring-authors-artists/. (October 10, 2019)

CHAPTER 5:

1. "Hearing the Voice of God with Rick Warren," YouTube video, 49:00, "Saddleback Church," Jul 7, 2015. https://www.youtube.com/watch?v=-MkxaUoFPbw
2. Meyer, Joyce. "You can Enjoy Your Life--Every Day!" Joyce Meyer. https://joycemeyer.org/everydayanswers/

ea-teachings/you-can-enjoy-your-life-every-day (October, 10 2019).

CHAPTER 6:

1. Persecuted--Dr. Charles Stanley," YouTube video, 49:01, "In Touch Ministries," Feb. 1, 2015. https://www.youtube.com/watch?v=kWgVo8LtNio&t=1970s

CHAPTER 8:

1. Rivers, Francine. "Writing Tips." Francine Rivers. https://francinerivers.com/writing-tips/ (October 10, 2019).

CHAPTER 10:

1. Ludy, Leslie. "Discovering Your True Identity." *Set Apart Girl.* Podcast audio, Oct. 15, 2017.

www.ingramcontent.com/pod-product-compliance
Lightning Source LLC
Chambersburg PA
CBHW071524180526
45171CB00002B/371